RENEWALS 458-4574

NEW DIRECTIONS FOR INSTITUTIONAL RESEARCH

J. Fredericks Volkwein, *Penn State University*
EDITOR-IN-CHIEF

Measuring What Matters

Competency-Based Learning Models in Higher Education

Richard A. Voorhees
Community Colleges of Colorado System

EDITOR

Number 110, Summer 2001

JOSSEY-BASS
San Francisco

MEASURING WHAT MATTERS: COMPETENCY-BASED LEARNING MODELS IN HIGHER EDUCATION
Richard A. Voorhees (ed.)
New Directions for Institutional Research, no. 110
Volume XXVIII, Number 2
J. Fredericks Volkwein, Editor-in-Chief

New Directions for Institutional Research is indexed in *College Student Personnel Abstracts, Contents Pages in Education,* and *Current Index to Journals in Education* (ERIC).

Microfilm copies of issues and chapters are available in 16mm and 35mm, as well as microfiche in 105mm, through University Microfilms Inc., 300 North Zeeb Road, Ann Arbor, Michigan 48106–1346.

ISSN 0271-0579   ISBN 0-7879-5782-8

NEW DIRECTIONS FOR INSTITUTIONAL RESEARCH is part of The Jossey-Bass Higher and Adult Education Series and is published quarterly by Jossey-Bass, 350 Sansome Street, San Francisco, California 94104-1342 (publication number USPS 098-830). Periodicals postage paid at San Francisco, California, and at additional mailing offices. POSTMASTER: Send address changes to New Directions for Institutional Research, Jossey-Bass, 350 Sansome Street, San Francisco, California 94104-1342.

SUBSCRIPTIONS cost $59.00 for individuals and $109.00 for institutions, agencies, and libraries.

EDITORIAL CORRESPONDENCE should be sent to J. Fredericks Volkwein, Center for the Study of Higher Education, Penn State University, 400 Rackley Building, University Park, PA 16801-5252.

Photograph of the library by Michael Graves at San Juan Capistrano by Chad Slattery © 1984. All rights reserved.

www.josseybass.com

Printed in the United States of America on acid-free recycled paper containing 100 percent recovered waste paper, of which at least 20 percent is postconsumer waste.

THE ASSOCIATION FOR INSTITUTIONAL RESEARCH was created in 1966 to benefit, assist, and advance research leading to improved understanding, planning, and operation of institutions of higher education. Publication policy is set by its Publications Committee.

For information about the Association for Institutional Research, write to the following address:

AIR Executive Office
114 Stone Building
Florida State University
Tallahassee, FL 32306-4462

(850) 644-4470

air@mailer.fsu.edu
http://airweb.org

CONTENTS

EDITOR'S NOTES

This *New Directions for Institutional Research* volume grows out of a recently concluded project commissioned by the National Postsecondary Education Cooperative (NPEC). That project sought to examine the data and policy implications of national skill standards, competency-based credentials, and assessment of work-based learning experiences across postsecondary education. The final report of that project (U.S. Department of Education, 2001) highlights out strong practices in competency-based initiatives among eight institutions and entities that are making the connection between competencies and the learning opportunities they seek to provide. The NPEC report provides an overview of overarching principles and strong practices in this area and complements the substance of this volume. Although the lessons learned from this effort are interspersed throughout the present volume, readers wishing a deeper understanding of the dynamics that accompany the implementation of competency based initiatives are encouraged to access the full report at nces.ed.gov/npec/products.html.

This volume provides researchers, faculty, and academic administrators with the tools they need to deal effectively with competencies. The techniques found here can help institutions foster the collaborations that are necessary to create competency-based learning models, to report competencies appropriately, and to match programs and curricula to labor markets.

This volume is divided into eight chapters. In Chapter One, I provide an overview of the emerging competency-based paradigm, detailing how and why it is critical to the future of U.S. higher education.

In Chapter Two, Elizabeth A. Jones presents techniques for institutional researchers and academic administrators to use in assisting faculty to implement competency-based learning strategies. Included here are recommendations on how competencies can be identified and how to approach consensus about expected levels of student performance as well as practical examples that illustrate how competencies can be developed. Drawing from the NPEC report, Jones identifies strong practices in transforming curricula as well as common pitfalls experienced by pioneering institutions.

The practical issues of measuring and reporting competencies are examined in Chapter Three. Trudy Bers examines the pursuit of common systems for counting, describing, and measuring competencies. Bers provides an overview of the role that validity and reliability play in the process of making competencies transportable, both within postsecondary education and outside it.

In Chapter Four, Karen Paulson examines the critical connections between the skills and competencies that employers seek and student preparation for them. Employers are increasingly skeptical of the skills possessed by graduates and have responded in some cases by creating their own training divisions, going as far as creating their own universities. Paulson suggests some of the fruitful connections that institutions might make with employers in the area of national skill standards and career transcripts.

One of the most difficult and controversial procedures in competency testing is the setting of appropriate passing standards for assessments. In Chapter Five, T. Dary Erwin and Steven L. Wise provide useful techniques for identifying a particular score, or standard, that differentiates competence from noncompetence. Institutional researchers will be very interested in the explicit procedures that they outline for developing appropriate standards that can assist institutions in resisting legal challenges when the results of testing are contested.

Chapter Six by Dawn GeronimoTerkla provides an overview of the connections between distance education, accreditation, and competencies. Distance education has grown in volume over the past five years. The paradigm that drives distance education is neither place-bound nor time-bound. Accordingly, as a natural test bed for competency-based learning models, it is increasingly recognized by regional and national accrediting bodies. The attraction of students to distance education from multiple providers, including unaccredited institutions, is forcing a dialogue about the very nature of certifying learning and portends transformation yet to come.

In Chapter Seven, Alice Bedard Voorhees presents a framework for creating competency-based models, including an analysis of the utility of national competency banks. These compilations of competencies offer many institutions a starting place and can save valuable time in implementing competency-based learning models. Implementation requires evaluation, and Bedard Voorhees presents a checklist that institutional researchers can use during and after the implementation phase to guide institutional success. This chapter concludes with a bibliography of selected Internet-based resources in the area of competency-based initiatives.

The volume concludes in Chapter Eight with a comprehensive bibliography on competencies by Karen Paulson. First appearing as part of the NPEC project, this bibliography is composed of five sections. The first is a general introduction to the history and basics of competencies in postsecondary education. The second contains citations about entry into postsecondary education, including competency-based admissions and placement. The third section of Paulson's bibliography focuses on the use of competencies in postsecondary education, such as competency-based curricula, general education competencies, and transfer competencies both within and across providers. Exit from postsecondary education, including end-of-program competencies, which are those used for employment placement and for admittance to graduate or professional schools, are found in the fourth section. The last section of Paulson's bibliography focuses on the use of competencies for overall institutional effectiveness, including program improvement, accountability, performance budgeting, and accreditation.

As a concluding note, this volume makes extensive use of Internet references. The Web sites cited throughout provide the most current compilations of competencies and developments in this emerging arena. Because these sites are frequently updated and occasionally relocated, however, readers will need to be ready to access search engines available within their own Web browser, as developments in this emerging field dictate. It is most likely that this burgeoning field will produce other Web sites that will provide an even more expanded set of resources for researchers, faculty, and academic administrators who choose to implement competencies in their institution's work.

Richard A. Voorhees
Editor

Reference

U.S. Department of Education, National Center for Education Statistics. *Defining and Assessing Learning: Exploring Competency-Based Initiatives* (by E. Jones, R. A. Voorhees, and K. Paulson for the Council of the National Postsecondary Education Cooperative Competency-Based Initiatives Working Group). Washington, D.C.: U.S. Department of Education, National Center for Education Statistics, 2001.

RICHARD A. VOORHEES *is associate vice president for instruction and student services for the Community Colleges of Colorado System.*

1

The pathways to learning no longer lead automatically to traditional institutions of higher education. Instead they lead most directly to learning opportunities in which competencies are defined explicitly and delivery options are multiple. This new paradigm will ultimately redefine the roles of faculty, institutions, and accreditors.

Competency-Based Learning Models: A Necessary Future

Richard A. Voorhees

We are in the early stages of a learning revolution. New learning pathways have been forged by intense competition from organizations whose sole purpose is to deliver learning (anytime and anywhere) and by rapid advances in information technology. Forged by expediency, these paths no longer lead automatically to institutions of higher education. Instead they lead most directly to learning opportunities that are intensely focused and are populated by learners and employers who are chiefly interested in the shortest route to results. In this paradigm, learning products are defined explicitly, delivery options are multiple, and a level of granularity not captured by traditional student transcripts (which display only credit hours and course titles) drives assessment. Most postsecondary institutions have been slow to accept these emerging realities, preferring instead to continue to package curricula in the standard lengths of the academic term and in traditional delivery formats. The bridge between the traditional paradigm, which depends on traditional credit hour measures of student achievement, and the learning revolution can be found in competency-based approaches. At a minimum, the shift in how potential students view their expanded learning options—especially issues connected to convenience—should cause most institutions to examine the menu of their current offerings. There is, however, often a considerable gap between intentions and actions. The difference creates an emerging field in which institutional researchers can play a major role.

The threat to traditional postsecondary institutions brought about by the movement toward competencies has not gone wholly unrecognized. The demand for certification of competencies that is not met by traditional higher educational providers defies measurement because there is no reporting mechanism for institutions that fall outside the U.S. Department of Education's Integrated Postsecondary Data System (IPEDS) from which to aggregate participation numbers. However, at least one source (Adelman, 2000) estimates the volume of worldwide certification in one employment sector—information technology—at 1.6 million between 1997 and 2000. These certifications, like others built to meet specific industry demand, are based solely on the learner's ability to demonstrate that specific competencies have been attained, regardless of where or even how they were mastered.

Institutional researchers and other campus administrators are probably very familiar with describing what their institutions produce in terms of *outcomes*. Student learning forms one distinct, but increasingly critical, corner of what most often are referred to as outcomes. Peter Ewell's (1985) edited *New Directions for Institutional Research* issue on assessing educational outcomes, now more than fifteen years old, remains this series' all-time bestseller. If anything, the interest in outcomes has accelerated over this time, as accountability schemes now in place in most states demand proof of institutional performance. This evidence is typically expressed in terms of retention rates, graduation rates, and placement rates—outcomes that typically are not direct measures of what students know or can accomplish. In contrast, competencies and the learning that they seek to measure operate at a much more granular level and require precise description and measurement of learning. Despite the advances and general interest in outcomes throughout higher education over the past decade, state indicator systems have only been able to approximate learning outcomes.

An International Movement

The interest in competencies and measuring specific learning is accelerating throughout the world. In the United States, interest in the skills needed for employment was heightened with the establishment of the National Skills Standards Board of the United States, an entity created under the Goals 2000: Educate America Act of 1994. Under this legislation, a twenty-eight-person board serves as a catalyst in the development and adoption of a voluntary national system of skill standards and of assessment and certification of attainment of skill standards. The Dearing Report (1997) captures the debate in the United Kingdom about lifelong learning and the necessity for portability of skills. An outgrowth of this study was the recent establishment of a quality assurance agency to work with institutions to establish small, expert teams to provide benchmark information on standards, in particular threshold standards, operating within the framework of qualifications. The result of these national discussions has been the establishment of the Learning Skills Council, a government partnership that is responsible for planning, funding, and improving the quality of post-sixteen, or postsecondary, learning up to university level, based on standards designed to provide articulation between educational providers and to provide a match between curriculum and employment opportunities.

Competencies and skill standards also have occupied considerable attention in Australia. Technical and further education (TAFE) courses provided by subuniversity providers offer programs leading to national qualifications. Several universities also offer TAFE programs, but because of their competency-based nature these programs do not appear to articulate well with university programs (Faris, 1995). New Zealand, in contrast, appears to address competency attainment from a wider perspective. The National Qualifications Framework in New Zealand contains eight different levels, leading ultimately to postgraduate certificates, diplomas, and degrees. This framework ensures that all students who meet the required standards, whether at schools or tertiary institutions, or in community, government, or private training establishments, or in the workplace, can gain recognition of their achievements (Faris, 1995).

One might surmise, at least from some of the foregoing discussion, that competencies are the exclusive domain of vocational education and that competency-based models have no application at baccalaureate-level or higher-level institutions. Early practice in the United States and aspirations in Europe would indicate otherwise. Of the five higher education institutions selected for study during the NPEC project (U.S. Department of Education, 2001), three were baccalaureates or higher institutions: Kings College, Northwest Missouri State University, and Western Governors University. Alverno College is often cited as a national model for competency-based baccalaureate education. Although it is true that the competency-based movement traces its roots to entities and institutions outside traditional four-year colleges and universities, especially community colleges, its benefits are beginning to be recognized by cutting-edge institutions, and the boundaries between sectors are becoming increasingly blurred. Voluntary standardization of content and corresponding length of degrees offered among European nations are also now under early discussion (Haug, 1999). These wide discussions have centered on the introduction of new curricula (instead of a mere repackaging of existing ones), a guaranteed level (gauged on the basis of knowledge and competencies acquired rather than time spent), and connections to the labor market.

A National Perspective on Assessing Learning

A recent report by the National Center for Public Policy and Higher Education (2000), entitled *Measuring Up 2000: The State-by-State Report Card for Higher Education,* was not able to grade student learning across the United States. This report, prepared by an independent national panel of experts, assigns traditional letter grades to each state, based on quantitative criteria. States were graded on preparation, participation, affordability, completion, and benefits. Each state, however, received an incomplete grade in student learning—conceptualized as measurable student learning at the end of lower-division study and again when students receive a baccalaureate degree, as well as the attainment of workplace skills. As Ewell explains, fewer than ten states administer a common test to a large number of college students (National Center for Public Policy and Higher Education, 2000, p. 174). The underlying reasons for lack of national benchmarking in student learning are even more complex. Coming to agreement on what core skills all college graduates ought to have is problematic, given the diversity of programs and institutions across the United States. Further, the creation of accurate assessments is not simple work. Employers and academicians alike agree that paper-and-pencil tests do not fully capture the complexity of performance that is commonly associated with college graduates. Ewell (2000) notes that the current inventory of national tests dates from the beginning of the national assessment movement, which began more than a decade ago. Considerable effort would need to be expended to create new assessments, some from scratch and some including new tests, which can address shortcomings in efforts to provide estimates of student learning. Of course, other factors limit state-by-state comparisons of student learning, including disparities in student motivation to score well and lack of political willpower and resources to adequately fund statewide testing. However, these issues are not likely to go away anytime soon, particularly given the emergence of a state-by-state report card and future efforts to incorporate student learning measures. Prudent institutional researchers will need to sharpen their awareness of these dynamics as well as their individual skills to be of value to their institutions as the national debate unfolds.

A Common Language

When dealing with learning outcomes, a common language set is critical. There are multiple definitions of student learning outcomes, objectives, skills, and ultimately the focus of this volume, competencies. To eliminate confusion, this volume uses the NPEC work group's definition of competency—namely, a *competency* is "a combination of skills, abilities, and knowledge needed to perform a specific task" (U.S. Department of Education, 2001, p. 1). The term *performance-based learning* is also used in this volume as a framework for learning systems that seek to document that a learner has attained a given competency or set of competencies. To aid the reader, Figure 1.1 depicts the hierarchical relationships between key terms used throughout this volume.

Figure 1.1 seeks to differentiate among terms commonly used in this area by depicting their interrelationships with competencies. Each of the rungs of this ladder is thought to influence those rungs that appear above and underneath. The first rung of this pyramid consists of *traits and characteristics*. These constitute the foundation for learning and depict the innate makeup of individuals on which further experiences can be built.

Figure 1.1. A Conceptual Learning Model

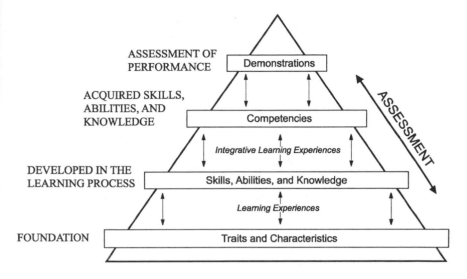

Source: U.S. Department of Education, 2001.

Differences in traits and characteristics help explain why people pursue different learning experiences and acquire different levels and kinds of skills, abilities, and knowledge. The second rung consists of *skills, abilities, and knowledge.* These are developed through learning experiences, broadly defined to include, among other possibilities, work and participation in community affairs. *Competencies,* then, are the result of integrative learning experiences in which skills, abilities, and knowledge interact to form learning bundles that have currency in relation to the task for which they are assembled. Finally, *demonstrations* are the results of applying competencies. It is at this level that performance-based learning can be assessed.

Bundling and Unbundling

A single competency can be used in many different ways. For example, measuring distances is important to both professional golfers and surveyors. Of course, different measuring skills may be involved in carrying out these two tasks, but the skill involved in performing measurement, irrespective of technique or method, should produce the same result. It is in their context, however, that competencies have their greatest utility. Competencies within different contexts require different *bundles* of skills and knowledge. It is this bundling and unbundling that drives competency-based initiatives among postsecondary entities. The challenge is to determine which competencies can be bundled together to provide different types of learners with the optimal combination of skills and knowledge needed to perform a specific task.

Leadership in a surgery suite is different from leadership on the basketball court. For example, motivating teammates is more important to leadership in basketball, whereas superior knowledge of the procedure is more important to leadership in surgery. In both contexts, however, an ability to effectively coordinate the roles, timing, and contributions of coworkers is critical. When skill bundles are labeled identically, there is often difficulty in achieving a common understanding of what a given competency (like leadership) is and then what it means to assess it. Knowing how to package the right set of competencies to effectively carry out a given task is in itself a competency. We sometimes refer to individuals as having great skills but seemingly being unable to apply them. With experience and experiment, people combine gestures, phrases, eye contact, pace of speech, and so forth in ways that allow them to give better speeches. It is easy to see that maturation, motivation, and opportunities to practice are keys to understanding the bundling and unbundling processes.

Obviously, one would do well not to mistake the definition and assessment of competencies for easy work. Efforts to define and assess competencies based on performance standards face a number of challenges. For example, what methodologies will be used to assess performance? Choices must be made among tests, portfolios, teacher or employer ratings, and benchmarks or exemplars of performance. Who will be responsible for assessment? Stakeholders and recipients of results must be defined among schools, admission offices, and employers. How will assessments of competencies be used? The potential uses (and misuses) by credentialing bodies, admissions and placement offices, and the recruitment arms of employers need careful consideration. These issues have ramifications for new data priorities as states and education and training providers encounter uncharted territory in developing performance standards and assessing competencies. This volume is intended to assist institutional researchers to identify the underlying as well as the more obvious issues in their efforts to assist others at their institutions to work with competencies.

Challenges to Competencies

In organizational life, all innovations foster resistance. Competency-based learning models are certainly no exception. Opponents view the movement toward competency-based systems, especially in general education areas, as reductionist and prescriptive (Betts and Smith, 1998). Nowhere is this controversy felt as much as in the assessment arena. There has been substantial progress and increased faculty involvement across higher education in assessment in the United States over the past decade. However, most of this activity is bounded and contained; it has been built on the assessment of academic programs, most often using the traditional course as the unit of analysis. It has not been conducted at the more malleable level of measurement necessitated by competencies. Course-based assessment always is dominated by the professional judgment of individual faculty. In contrast, competency-based learning models most often rely on the judgment of those external to the learning process and employ assessment strategies that are based on units of analysis that are smaller, and certainly more granular and addressable, than those used to assess traditional courses.

Competency-based models ultimately rely on measurable assessment. In other words, if a proposed competency cannot be described unambiguously and subsequently measured, it probably is not a competency. Given these fundamental attributes, all parties to the learning process—faculty, external experts, administrators, and students—should be able to understand with clarity the outcomes of the learning experience. Under these circumstances, competencies are transparent. Learning outcomes hold no mystery, and faculty are freed from the burden of defending learning outcomes that are verified only by professional judgment.

There are clear advantages for students in competency-based learning models. Because learning can be described and measured in ways that are apprehended by all parties, competencies permit the learner to return to one or more competencies that have not been mastered in a learning process rather than facing the unwelcome prospect of repeating one or more traditional courses. Competencies also provide students with a clear map and the navigational tools needed to move expeditiously toward their goals. In an ideal world, competencies would logically and clearly build on other competencies. In this world, time horizons become more manageable, providing students with certain flexibility. The current architecture of higher education in the United States does not easily promote the open exchange of learner competencies across sectors—for example, community colleges to four-year colleges and universities—and between providers—for example, nonaccredited institutions to accredited institutions. In the meantime, institutions and students are often left to navigate issues of transportability of learning experiences in uncharted waters.

Faculty and administrators, too, would realize more flexibility and options in educational delivery systems. These options, though, require fundamental reengineering of current delivery systems, inviting debate about the traditional academic structure, the standard length of academic terms, and the very process for certifying student learning. In many important ways, competency-based systems have the potential to redistribute the power relationships between teachers and those taught (Betts and Smith, 1998). Fortunately, there exists some practical guidance to those institutions that wish to pursue competency-based models.

Strong Practices

The NPEC report sought to provide practitioners and policymakers with a hands-on guide to developing, implementing, or refining competency-based learning models. This sourcebook draws on the strong practices identified from the case studies found in this final report (U.S. Department of Education, 2001). These practices are identified in the following list. At first blush, the accumulation of these principles together may seem overwhelming to faculty and administrators who are wondering whether to create a competency-based system. However, the NPEC working group examined at least some institutions that have been working at competency-based learning models for many years. Accordingly, although the following list may seem overwhelming, it is drawn from achievements over many years. One of the greatest overriding lessons learned from the NPEC work is to provide sufficient amounts of time and guidance to help faculty develop, implement, and evaluate their competency-based educational initiative. The strong practices uncovered in the NPEC research (U.S. Department of Education, 2001) include these fundamentals:

* A senior administrator is the public advocate, leader, and facilitator for creating an institutional culture that is open to change, is willing to take risks, and fosters innovations by providing real incentives for participants.
* The appropriate stakeholders fully participate in identifying, defining, and reaching consensus about important competencies.
* Competencies are clearly defined, understood, and accepted by relevant stakeholders.
* Competencies are defined at a sufficient level of specificity that they can be assessed.
* Multiple assessments of competencies provide useful and meaningful information that is relevant to the decision-making and policy development contexts.
* Faculty and staff fully participate in making decisions about the strongest assessment instruments that will measure their specific competencies.
* Precision, reliability, validity, credibility, and costs are all considered and examined in making selections of the best commercially developed assessments or locally developed assessment approaches.
* The competency-based educational initiative is embedded in a larger institutional planning process.
* The assessments of competencies are directly linked with the goals of the learning experience.
* The assessment results are used in making critical decisions about strategies to improve student learning.
* The assessment results are clear and are reported in a meaningful way so that all relevant stakeholders fully understand the findings.
* The institution experiments with new ways to document students' mastery of competencies that supplement the traditional transcript.

References

Adelman, C. *A Parallel Postsecondary Universe: The Certification System in Information Technology.* Washington, D.C.: U.S. Department of Education, Office of Educational Research and Improvement, 2000.

Betts, M., and Smith, R. *Developing the Credit-Based Modular Curriculum in Higher Education.* Bristol, Pa.: Falmer Press, 1998.

Dearing, R. *Higher Education in the Learning Society: Report of the National Committee.* London: Her Majesty's Stationery Office, 1997. [www.ex.ac.uk/dearing.html].

Ewell, P. T. (ed.). *Assessing Educational Outcomes.* New Directions for Institutional Research, no. 47. San Francisco: Jossey-Bass, 1985.

Ewell, P. T. "Grading Student Learning: Better Luck Next Time." In National Center for Public Policy and Higher Education (ed.), *Measuring Up 2000: The State-by-State Report Card for Higher Education.* San Jose, Calif.: National Center for Public Policy and Higher Education, 2000. [www.highereducation.org].

Faris, R. *Major Reforms in Training Systems in Three Countries.* Victoria, Canada: Ministry of Skills, Training and Labour, 1995.

Haug, R. "Trends in Learning Structures in Higher Education in Europe." Paper prepared for the Confederation of European Rectors conferences and the Association of European Universities, Aug. 1999. [www.rks.dk/trends3.htm].

National Center for Public Policy and Higher Education. *Measuring Up 2000: The State-by-State Report Card for Higher Education.* San Jose, Calif.: National Center for Public Policy and Higher Education, 2000. [www.highereducation.org].

U.S. Department of Education, National Center for Education Statistics. *Defining and Assessing Learning: Exploring Competency-Based Initiatives* (by E. Jones, R. A. Voorhees, and K. Paulson for the Council of the National Postsecondary Education Cooperative Competency-Based Initiatives Working Group). Washington, D.C.: U.S. Department of Education, National Center for Education Statistics, 2001.

RICHARD A. VOORHEES is associate vice president for instruction and student services for the Community Colleges of Colorado System.

2

There are many opportunities for institutional researchers to work with faculty to create competency-based learning models. This chapter explores specific techniques that benefit faculty, institutional researchers, and, ultimately, students.

Working in Partnership with Faculty to Transform Undergraduate Curricula

Elizabeth A. Jones

Widespread concern about the quality of undergraduate student learning dominates the higher education community. Since the 1980s, a steady stream of reports has called for reforms and improvements (for example, Association of American Colleges, 1985; Bloom, 1987; Boyer and Kaplan, 1977; Boyer and Levine, 1981; Carnegie Foundation for the Advancement of Teaching, 1977). Each has urged faculty and administrators to make not merely marginal changes in the curricula but rather fundamental reforms that would make significant differences in student learning. The Wingspread Group on Higher Education (1993, p. 14), for example, believed that learning should be the "heart of the academic enterprise" and would necessitate "overhauling the conceptual, procedural, curricular, and other architecture of postsecondary education on most campuses." They recommended that institutions define learning (what students need to succeed), then set higher expectations for all students and help them reach these outcomes. Rigorous assessments were viewed as the key to determining what students know and are able to do in order to strengthen both student and institutional performance. The Boyer Commission (1998) called for more opportunities for undergraduates to learn through inquiry rather than simple transmission of knowledge. They also stressed the importance of "training in the skills necessary for oral and written communication at a level that will serve the student both within the university and in postgraduate professional and personal life" (Boyer Commission, 1998, p. 12).

The purpose of this chapter is to discuss the specific issues related to defining and embedding competencies across courses and other learning experiences with the intentions of enhancing student performance. Drawing

New Directions for Institutional Research, no. 110, Summer 2001   © John Wiley & Sons, Inc.   15 from a recent national study of competency-based initiatives in postsecondary education (U.S. Department of Education, 2001), this chapter will provide suggestions and strategies for faculty and institutional researchers who want to work collaboratively to improve student learning.

Why Is It Important to Articulate Student Learning Outcomes?

Institutional or program goals articulated in college catalogues are often expressed broadly, inclusive of important concepts such as developing character, citizenship, or cultural appreciation. Although these institutional goals are laudable, they also are ambiguous and provide insufficient direction about the desired levels of student achievement. To provide institutional direction and cohesion, it is necessary to state competencies or objectives that can be used as building blocks en route to overarching education goals. Sometimes used synonymously, the terms *objectives* or *competencies* should be expressed as statements that indicate the specific skills and knowledge that undergraduates should develop. At this level of granularity, *competency statements* also provide sufficient information about expected student performance that can guide their assessment. Constructed in this manner, competency statements form an institution's expectations for student learning.

Across general education and in some fields of specialization, the articulation of specific learning competencies is a major challenge because faculty tend to organize the curriculum and course of study around the presentation of content rather than on building specific skills across the curriculum. Students in the arts and sciences fields are socialized "not only into the rhetoric of the discipline but also into the operational assumption that they have no need or responsibility to integrate their learning across multiple domains of inquiry and practice" (Schneider and Shoenberg, 1999, p. 31). The development of writing skills across many institutions is viewed as the responsibility of the English department, and students are expected to attain these skills through one or two introductory writing courses. Similarly, students are typically expected to learn about speech communication by enrolling in one general education course. Given the increasing importance of crossing boundaries and exploring connections, students need to practice and apply these skills across their entire undergraduate experiences. Concrete statements about the intended results of individual courses, general education, and major programs, including the development of communication, critical thinking, and problem-solving skills across the curriculum, are essential for determining whether students have attained needed competencies.

Even though many program faculty and general education committees find defining goals and objectives to be a difficult part of the assessment process, they also find it to be the most productive part (Wolff, 1990). Structured, ongoing dialogues among faculty about educational goals, objectives, and criteria can create a culture with an emphasis on learning outcomes. Such a learning culture brings to the forefront important assumptions of individual faculty that are often never discussed with colleagues. Decisions about appropriate competencies and levels of learning with some degree of consensus among faculty (for example, within a particular major) can lead to greater clarity, coherence, and focus within academic programs and general education.

Embarking on the path to assessments of student learning is a long-term journey that requires many important decisions, such as the choice of appropriate measures and methods to evaluate outcomes. If faculty do not know what they are trying to achieve, then it is difficult to know whether they are accomplishing it. When faculty articulate specific competencies, they then have clear information that can guide decisions about the most appropriate and relevant assessments at the course, program, and institutional levels. When faculty have worked through a consensus-building process about important competencies, it is likely that they have also developed a common understanding about the specific skills and knowledge that undergraduates should master. Faculty, employers, students, and policymakers will therefore not only understand desired competencies, they will also be more likely to accept and value them. Finally, agreement about specific competency statements provides direction for designing learning experiences and assignments that will help students gain practice at using and applying these competencies in different contexts.

In order to transform the undergraduate curriculum, faculty and institutional researchers need to work in partnership to formally identify the particular competencies that are essential for their own students by surveying or interviewing relevant constituency groups. These groups may include current faculty, undergraduate students, alumni, and employers of the program's graduates. Once faculty review and evaluate these research results, they can make informed decisions about which particular competencies are most important for their undergraduates. Institutional researchers can also help by providing faculty with techniques to gauge the validity and reliability of their assessments. Specific examples of these techniques are found later in this chapter.

Faculty may choose more informal strategies to gain feedback about important competencies. For example, a department chair may take a small group of students to lunch and ask them for feedback about their own learning and development. An advisory board may be convened once a year to give advice about the direction of the program and its quality. These types of strategies can be helpful and may supplement more rigorous, formal approaches, but they should not be the sole basis for making important decisions because typically only a small number of individuals are informally consulted, raising concerns about validity and reliability.

Strategies for Identifying Important Competencies and Reaching Consensus

Once faculty decide to review their curriculum, a first step is to evaluate whether relevant, current competencies that are needed to be successful in the real world have been articulated. Despite major advances in institutional research and analysis, some individuals continue to find it difficult to use data and research results in their decision-making processes (Chaffee, 1990). Although it may be tempting to make decisions about relevant competencies by using intuition, imitation, or even sporadic discussions, formal research strategies can be employed to identify the relevant competencies. It is here that institutional researchers can play a key role.

In professional programs such as business, nursing, or engineering, the connections between program competencies and successful employment are very clear. Professional accrediting organizations usually articulate prescriptive guidelines about the specific competencies that professional programs must embed in their courses and majors. In addition, graduates of these programs often must pass certifying examinations developed by practitioners in conjunction with professional associations. Also, these outcomes are directly influenced by regional accreditation requirements.

Institutional researchers and faculty can draw on existing research-based resources that have defined and outlined relevant competencies. Several representative competency banks are reviewed, and examples of two formal strategies to work with appropriate groups of faculty and other individuals to reach a consensus about the most important competencies are provided.

Sources of Existing Information About Specific Competencies

It is prudent to review and evaluate multiple, external sources of information about relevant competencies prior to settling on specific competencies. Resources that define competencies arise from extensive national research studies conducted in the United States. Some of this research is specific to workforce development and technical programs, whereas other studies are focused on the development of lifelong-learning competencies.

In recent history, workers had jobs that were limited and well-defined. They performed a set of routine tasks by following specific instructions. Today high-performance organizations are requiring new sets of skills, and workers are now expected to integrate their skills to solve complex problems, find ways to strengthen their methods, and work in teams. In 1991, the Secretary's Commission on Achieving Necessary Skills (SCANS) attempted to break away from the traditional approaches to articulating workplace competencies and address the necessity of integrating skills common to all occupations as well as those competencies unique to particular jobs (Bailey and

Merritt, 1995). SCANS gathered nationally recognized experts to analyze the requirements of innovative work environments and emerging technologies.

SCANS competencies include the "basic skills (reading, writing, arithmetic and mathematics, and speaking and listening); thinking skills (reasoning, thinking creatively, making decisions, and solving problems); and personal qualities (individual responsibility and self-management, sociability, and integrity)" (Secretary's Commission on Achieving Necessary Skills, 1993, p. 6; see also Secretary's Commission on Achieving Necessary Skills, 1992). These competencies also consist of workplace outcomes, which include resources (allocating time, money, materials, space, and staff); interpersonal skills (working in teams, teaching others, serving customers, negotiating, and working well with people from diverse backgrounds); information (acquiring and evaluating data, organizing and maintaining files, interpreting and communicating, and using computers to process information); systems (understanding social, organizational, and technological systems, monitoring and correcting performance, and designing or improving systems); and technology (selecting equipment and tools, applying technology to specific tasks, and maintaining and troubleshooting equipment). SCANS competencies are most frequently used or adapted by community colleges because they offer the technical programs most closely associated with these types of competencies.

Industry-based skills standards also are the focus of reforms in technical programs (Bailey and Merritt, 1995). In 1994, the Goals 2000: Educate America Act established the National Skills Standards Board (NSSB) to encourage, promote, and assist in the voluntary development and adoption of a national system of voluntary industry-based skills standards (Bailey and Merritt, 1995). The NSSB has categorized the workforce into fifteen industry sectors (see www.nssb.org/briefdescription.htm), and two sectors (manufacturing and retail-wholesale industries) are nearing the completion of developing skill standards. In effect, these standards serve to define specific competencies that students should achieve in technical programs at the associate and certificate levels.

Another major study conducted by Rothwell, Sanders, and Soper (2000) clusters competencies considered important for working professionals (who have often completed baccalaureate degrees). In this study, 1,031 employers (representing different industries, disciplines, and positions) evaluated the importance of competencies linked to seven specific professional workplace roles: manager, analyst, intervention designer and developer, intervention implementer, change leader, and evaluator. Analytical competencies associated with creating new understandings or methods through the synthesis of multiple ideas, processes, and data were very important. Business competencies associated with the understanding of organizations as systems were rated highly. Interpersonal competencies focused on understanding and applying methods that produce effective interaction between individuals and groups were critical. Leadership competencies, such as influencing, enabling, or inspiring others to act, were important. Technical competencies consist of understanding and applying existing knowledge or processes. Finally, technological competencies are associated with understanding and applying appropriate applications of current or emerging technologies.

The National Center for Education Statistics funded a series of studies to identify the specific skills that undergraduates (including associate and baccalaureate degree students) should master in communications (writing, critical reading, speaking, listening), problem solving, and critical thinking. Major outcomes from this research are five different goals inventories (Jones, 1996), which encompass the ideal skills that college graduates should achieve. These comprehensive frameworks highlight skills that cut across general education and academic programs, so faculty can review a potential array of important competencies and then decide which specific skills are most important.

Formal Strategies to Reach a Consensus

When potential competencies have been identified, then the best strategy for getting formal feedback from various constituencies, including faculty, alumni, current undergraduate students, and employers who hire the program's graduates, should be selected. The strategies outlined here are research based and require a formal analysis of results for the produced information to be meaningful, useful, and valid. Faculty leaders may decide to either interview relevant stakeholder groups or survey them, or they may decide to use both strategies. Clearly, these research-based approaches are important activities that would benefit greatly from institutional researchers' working collaboratively with faculty members.

Using DACUM. One productive approach to formally identifying important competencies is the strategy of developing a curriculum (DACUM), which is used for guiding the formal analysis of positions or occupations at the professional, managerial, technical, skilled, and semi-skilled levels. DACUM is based on three assumptions (Norton, 1998). First, expert workers can describe and define their job or occupation more accurately then anyone else. Typically, individuals who are working full-time in their positions are the experts in their positions who can provide a high-quality analysis of important competencies. The second assumption is that important competencies can be identified by considering the nature of particular jobs and describing the tasks that expert workers perform. Successful employees typically perform a wide range of tasks that are needed by the employer and customer. New workers who possess only solid technical skills are no longer sufficient. For example, accountants may be experts in auditing principles, but such professionals will also need strong communication and problem-solving skills to be effective in their field. Third, the tasks that employees perform require the use of a combination of certain knowledge, skills, tools, attitudes, and behaviors. Attitudes such as being open-minded or behaviors such as reporting to work on time are not specific tasks, but they are nonetheless important because they motivate the employee to perform at a high level. As attributes are different from tasks, it is also important to include them in an analysis of relevant competencies.

Typically, a group of six to twelve experts, individuals who have actually performed these tasks and jobs under investigation, are selected to carefully review and analyze the necessary knowledge, skills, and attitudes. A trained facilitator leads the group through a two-day brainstorming process. The group primarily identifies general areas of responsibility, pinpoints specific tasks performed in connection with each duty, reviews and refines the tasks and duty statements, sequences them, and identifies entry-level tasks (Norton, 1987, p. 15). The group is also charged with articulating the essential behaviors, attitudes, and knowledge that workers need to successfully perform their jobs. A DACUM chart is developed, which provides a graphic display of the tasks involved in a certain job.

After the chart has been developed, it is usually validated by a second group of experts. This group reviews the chart to determine if the tasks are entry level, if they are important for the particular occupation, how frequently the tasks are performed, and if certain tasks are missing. The DACUM chart is then revised based on feedback from the second group, and it becomes the foundation for developing or revising the associated curriculum. The result is a validated job model based on the views of exemplary performers (Rothwell, 2000). It is more specific than a job description, and it reflects what individuals state they actually perform in their jobs rather than what others believe they do or what others state they should do. DACUM has also been used to conceptualize the requirements for future jobs and to design educational programs for certain professions or occupations (Norton, 1998).

Some college and university faculty have used a shorter version of the DACUM process, in which the group of experts begins with an *existing* task list and modifies or verifies the tasks on the list. Consequently, it can be accomplished in less than one day, compared with the two days required in the more developmental DACUM strategy (Norton, 1997). The main difference from the traditional DACUM process is that the actual workers themselves are often not involved in this process. Instead employers or supervisors indicate what is important based on their own perceptions and experiences working with employees.

Faculty in the community college consortium spearheaded by Johns Hopkins University used a modified DACUM process to grapple with the competency-setting process. For about one year, a panel of seventeen employers met four times with another panel of fifteen educators representing the nation's community colleges. This length of time was necessary to promote a full discussion and review of potential outcomes. In addition, the necessary and appropriate stakeholder groups were directly participating in the identification and consensus-reaching processes. Ultimately, these panels recommended that the SCANS competencies be adopted.

Using the Delphi Approach. A second research-based approach to identifying important competencies is the Delphi approach. This strategy has been used for planning in higher education settings to improve communication and reach consensus about a variety of issues (Uhl, 1971, 1983). In this process, leaders usually solicit nominations to get the best experts to make informed judgments. Experts usually complete several rounds of surveys, and after each round researchers analyze the results to identify the items with agreements and those items with significant disagreements. For example, faculty, employers, and alumni may be asked to rate the importance of specific skills. Institutional researchers can perform an analysis of variance for each item to determine if there are significant differences in the mean responses across groups. Subsequent survey rounds ask respondents to again rate the importance of those items on which there were significant disagreements and to take the opportunity to revise their previous responses. In each subsequent round, participants are provided with the results from the previous round, often expressed as the mean score for each item, and given the opportunity to express disagreements by writing comments. The main goal is to reach a consensus through successive iterations of the survey.

The DACUM and Delphi approaches can provide powerful consensus-building strategies for faculty because they are based on structured analyses and encourage faculty to openly express their own conflicting viewpoints. When all faculty participants have a part in the decision-making process, they are more likely to accept and value the results. The desired end in these processes is a revised curriculum in which new courses are created, others are revised, and some courses are eliminated. The ultimate goal is that "blocks of courses will be designated in specific sequences to build upon students' knowledge and skills" (Connolly and Dotson, 1996, p. 15).

Whereas the DACUM process is usually conducted with small focus groups and relies on the expertise of a skilled facilitator, the Delphi technique is a useful tool because it helps larger groups (potentially hundreds) of diverse individuals reach a collective judgment about the important competencies. Through a formal survey process, participants can objectively reflect on an array of skills and decide which ones are most important in their environment. The outcomes of this work are more likely to be accepted and deemed credible if more people participate in the exploration and definition processes than if the work is conducted in personal or group interviews and meetings.

Institutional researchers should be prepared to lend statistical expertise to help faculty design their surveys so that the items are clear and make sense. In addition, it is important to construct a meaningful scale for participants to use in their evaluations. Institutional researchers can help faculty design their sampling plans so that they get an adequate and representative sample of the necessary stakeholder groups. Given the potentially large volume of quantitative data, institutional researchers should work closely with faculty to ensure that the statistical techniques are followed and reported accurately. In combination, these institutional research activities can considerably strengthen the process of establishing competencies that are reliable and valid.

Linking Competencies with the Learning Process

Once faculty have identified relevant and valid competencies for their undergraduate students, they are ready to either create or redesign their existing courses and academic programs to address these competencies. Competencies can have a stronger impact on student learning when they are linked and embedded within specific courses and across both general education and academic majors. Consideration should be given to whether certain competencies will cut across all academic programs, including general education, or whether certain competencies are specific to disciplines. Generic competencies, such as writing, oral communication, critical thinking, and problem solving, can and should cut across academic programs.

Faculty and academic leaders at King's College grappled with these issues (U.S. Department of Education, 2001). They were dissatisfied with the distribution of general education across the curriculum, believing it produced fragmented learning experiences. Their solution was to design a new general education curriculum focused on competencies. All new courses were created by project teams composed of faculty from more than one discipline (Farmer, 1999b). These teams were empowered to make recommendations and to implement the changes into action. The academic vice president deliberately developed teams rather than committees because traditional committees are often viewed by faculty and others in a negative way, as they often emphasize protecting the territorial interests of their own department or academic programs (Farmer, 1999a). Also, committees frequently make recommendations and then depend on others to implement the ideas. In contrast, teams are more fully committed to conceptualizing new ideas and then actually strive to incorporate actions into the culture of the institution. At King's College, faculty teams agreed that general education and all academic programs would be designed to help undergraduates develop the following specific skills: critical thinking, effective writing, effective oral communication, library and information literacy, creative thinking and problem solving, moral reasoning, computer literacy, and quantitative reasoning.

All courses in the general education curriculum were designed for nonmajors. The faculty believed that this new curriculum is vital to promote a stronger coherence and integrity of knowledge. Each liberal-learning category had clear goals and specific objectives for all courses that constitute the curriculum. These goals and objectives included numerous connections between the liberal-learning categories.

King's College faculty believed that an undergraduate education helps students view learning as cumulative, transferable, and integrative. To effect this vision, competency-growth plans for each academic program were developed, defining each crosscutting liberal-learning skill in the context of the major. Each liberal-learning skill was then divided into specific competencies for students to develop from their beginning freshman through senior years in both general education and major courses. Each competency-growth plan included a definition of each competency, an indication of courses and assignments that were designed to help students develop the competency, and specific criteria that faculty and students used to gauge the quality of student performance. These plans become guides for faculty and students so they know what can be expected from different courses and what competency linkages are important.

These main competencies are reinforced in course syllabi and translated into individual course assignments. Faculty reporting requirements were instituted by the academic leaders to ensure that students were mastering the important competencies, and these plans are shared with all colleagues to foster a common understanding of how competencies are developed across the curriculum. The reported assessment results must include a description of the following: course-embedded assessment activities, criteria given to students in writing before the assessment; samples of student performance at three levels (superior, satisfactory, and less than satisfactory but still acceptable); a report of the number of students performing at each level; and an explanation of how assessment results will be shared with faculty on a project team or in the department and with students (King's College, 1999, p. 32).

As all program faculty are required to complete these competency-growth plans and share them with others, stakeholders have a clear understanding of expectations and linkages across courses, programs, and general education, too. Students realize that skills such as critical thinking and effective writing will be expected and built on in numerous courses in their academic majors and will not be confined exclusively to their general education curriculum.

At Northwest Missouri State University, faculty decided that they wanted to develop and implement their own assessment of students' writing skills after students had completed the required course sequence. They created a series of short, related readings (from newspapers or magazines) about a controversial topic and then asked students to respond to specific prompts. Faculty designed a rubric to assess specific dimensions of student writing that they thought were important. Specific competencies were identified for the organization of the paper, its development, language, and documentation. These specific expectations were then divided into three levels of quality: excellent, adequate, and inadequate. Faculty were trained about how to assess student writing using the developed rubric. They initially reviewed a sample of students' work to determine how close their ratings were to one another's scores. If there are wide discrepancies, they then discuss their reasons for scoring student writing in a certain way. Once a fairly high level of consistency is reached through this training process, two faculty members read each student's end-of-core writing assessment. If there are major disagreements for a particular essay, a third reader scores it, and this brings closure to the assessment. The formal training process of all raters and the use of an agreed-upon rubric have helped faculty achieve greater reliability in their judgments about the quality of student writing. In addition, the use of a real-world problem presented from the context of several different sources of information helped students examine an issue and justify their own solutions.

Faculty who decide to explore the creation of a competency-based model should consider and answer the following questions as they determine how to link the competencies with the learning experiences: Where in the curriculum will students learn and practice skills such as writing, critical thinking, speaking, and teamwork? What teaching strategies and assignments will be given to students to help them develop these skills? What types of assessments will be selected to determine if students are mastering the competencies? What types of skills should be required across courses in general education and all majors? What levels of performance should be expected (a minimum level or different levels of mastery)? When faculty reflect on, discuss, and answer these questions, they can clearly demonstrate their plans through formal documentation that is completed and shared with relevant stakeholder groups.

Although faculty are the key decision makers about curricular issues, they generally lack training in building strong assessments. Institutional researchers can be particularly helpful as faculty explore what types of assessments are best and actually measure the intended competencies. Institutional researchers can help faculty review commercially developed instruments as well as critique locally developed approaches, with a particular emphasis on reliability and validity. T. Dary Erwin and Steven L. Wise's chapter in this volume provides institutional researchers with the background to assist faculty to make appropriate decisions about where to set cutoff scores for assessment instruments. Many faculty have not been trained to evaluate the quality of different instruments, especially when it comes to measuring their own competencies rather than only those set by the testing companies.

Disappointingly few sites in the NPEC competency-based initiatives study (U.S. Department of Education, 2001) were actively dealing with issues of reliability and validity. Instead, as might be expected of relatively new endeavors, issues of process and internal acceptance for competencies were the initial focus, taking time, energy, and resources. As postsecondary institutions gain more experience with competency-based initiatives, a focus on validity and reliability will be important. By attending to such concerns, institutions can glean meaningful information to improve their initiatives and to satisfy external demands for accountability.

Conclusion

Given the advantages of the approaches discussed in this chapter, it seems prudent to recommend that faculty and academic leaders should create and implement competency-based education. Such a path represents a major transformation for most institutions that is complex but manageable. There are many important considerations, and this chapter has presented some techniques to make this pursuit stronger and more manageable. Institutional researchers can offer faculty significant expertise as they attempt to identify and define important competencies as well as assess them. Particularly important for effective faculty and institutional researcher collaboration are issues of reliability and validity. Again, institutional researchers can help faculty determine if their competencies are valid and essential. They can also assist with evaluating the quality of instruments and determining the consistency of results over time and whether they are valid.

Formal research techniques are needed even at the beginning stages of program planning and development. Although it may seem easier to hold a few informal conversations with colleagues, such information will not usefully guide the future directions of academic programs. When formal research techniques are used in the very beginning and throughout the planning and implementation stages, then faculty and other stakeholders know that they will have meaningful data that can inform and shape the future directions of their curriculum. Data from formal research can help faculty discover if students are mastering the important competencies.

References

Association of American Colleges. *Integrity in the College Curriculum: A Report to the Academic Community.* Washington, D.C.: Association of American Colleges, 1985.

Bailey, T., and Merritt, D. *Making Sense of Industry-Based Skill Standards.* Berkeley, Calif.: National Center for Research in Vocational Education, 1995. (CE 070 410)

Bloom, A. *The Closing of the American Mind.* New York: Simon & Schuster, 1987.

Boyer Commission on Educating Undergraduates in the Research University. *Reinventing Undergraduate Education: A Blueprint for America's Research Universities.* Menlo Park, Calif.: Carnegie Foundation for the Advancement of Teaching, 1998.

Boyer, E. L., and Kaplan, M. *Educating for Survival.* New Rochelle, N.Y.: Change Magazine Press, 1977.

Boyer, E. L., and Levine, A. *A Quest for Common Learning.* Menlo Park, Calif.: Carnegie Foundation for the Advancement of Teaching, 1981.

Carnegie Foundation for the Advancement of Teaching. *Missions of the College Curriculum: A Contemporary Review with Suggestions.* San Francisco: Jossey-Bass, 1977.

Chaffee, E. E. "Strategies for the 1990s." In L. W. Jones and F. A. Nowotny (eds.), *An Agenda for the New Decade.* New Directions for Higher Education, no. 70. San Francisco: Jossey-Bass, 1990.

Connolly, M., and Dotson, M. "Using Action Research to Inform Curriculum Deliberation in an Early Childhood Education Teacher Education Program." Paper presented at the annual conference of the Mid-Western Educational Research Association, Chicago, Oct. 1996.

Farmer, D. W. "Course-Embedded Assessment: A Catalyst for Realizing the Paradigm Shift from Teaching to Learning." *Journal of Staff, Program, and Organizational Development*, 1999a, *16*(4), 199–211.

Farmer, D. W. "Institutional Improvement and Motivated Faculty: A Case Study." In M. Theall (ed.), *Motivation from Within: Approaches for Encouraging Faculty and Students to Excel*. New Directions for Teaching and Learning, no. 78. San Francisco: Jossey-Bass, 1999b.

Jones, E. A. *Goals Inventories*. University Park, Pa.: National Center on Postsecondary Teaching, Learning, and Assessment, 1996.

King's College. *King's College Periodic Review Report* (submitted to the Middle States Association of Colleges and Schools). Wilkes-Barre, Pa.: King's College, 1999.

Norton, R. E. "A Tool for Developing Curricula." *Vocational Education Journal*, 1987, *62*(3), 15.

Norton, R. E. *DACUM Handbook*. (2nd ed.) Columbus: Ohio State University, 1997.

Norton, R. E. *Quality Instruction for the High Performance Workplace: DACUM*. Columbus: Ohio State University, 1998. (ED 419 155)

Rothwell, W. J. *The Analyst: Workplace Learning and Performance Roles*. Alexandria, Va.: American Society for Training and Development, 2000.

Rothwell, W. J., Sanders, E. S., and Soper, J. G. *American Society for Training and Development Models for Workplace Learning and Performance: Roles, Competencies, and Outputs*. Alexandria, Va.: American Society for Training and Development, 2000.

Schneider, C. G., and Shoenberg, R. "Habits Hard to Break: How Persistent Features of Campus Life Frustrate Curricular Reform." *Change*, Mar.–Apr. 1999, *31*(2), 30–35.

Secretary's Commission on Achieving Necessary Skills. *What Work Requires of Schools: A SCANS Report for America 2000*. Washington, D.C.: U.S. Department of Labor, 1991.

Secretary's Commission on Achieving Necessary Skills. *Blueprint for High Performance*. Washington, D.C.: U.S. Department of Labor, 1992.

Secretary's Commission on Achieving Necessary Skills. *Teaching the SCANS Competencies*. Washington, D.C.: U.S. Department of Labor, 1993.

Uhl, N. P. *Encouraging Convergence of Opinion Through the Use of the Delphi Technique in the Process of Identifying an Institution's Goals*. Princeton, N.J.: Educational Testing Service, 1971.

Uhl, N. P. "Using the Delphi Technique in Institutional Planning." In N. P. Uhl (ed.), *Using Research for Strategic Planning*. New Directions for Institutional Research, no. 37. San Francisco: Jossey-Bass, 1983.

U.S. Department of Education, National Center for Education Statistics. *Defining and Assessing Learning: Exploring Competency-Based Initiatives* (by E. Jones, R. A. Voorhees, and K. Paulson for the Council of the National Postsecondary Education Cooperative Competency-Based Initiatives Working Group). Washington, D.C.: U.S. Department of Education, National Center for Education Statistics, 2001.

Wingspread Group on Higher Education. *An American Imperative: Higher Expectations for Higher Education*. Racine, Wis.: Johnson Foundation, 1993.

Wolff, R. A. "Assessment and Accreditation: A Shotgun Marriage?" In T. Marchese (ed.), *Assessment 1990: Accreditation and Renewal*. Washington, D.C.: American Association for Higher Education, 1990.

ELIZABETH A. JONES is assistant professor of higher education leadership at West Virginia University.

3

Competency-based learning models create unusual data and reporting demands that may not integrate well with traditional systems. These implications should be considered as institutions begin planning for these models.

Measuring and Reporting Competencies

Trudy H. Bers

Measuring and reporting competencies requires new and innovative processes. At the same time, the fundamentals of measurement, such as validity and reliability, feasibility of data collection and maintenance, and effective ways to analyze and report results, must be built into any new approach to documenting student learning in useful ways. The data implications of competency-based educational programs are important both for evaluating programs and for conveying meaningful information about students' performances. It is important for educators to grapple with these implications when they first begin to consider planning and implementing competency-based programs. Embarking on this path creates new and unusual data and reporting demands. These demands will not integrate well with traditional systems for recording and reporting student learning outcomes.

This chapter reviews the types of data issues that will be encountered by institutions offering competency-based learning models. It also offers some examples of how colleges have addressed these issues. Before turning to this discussion, however, a basic definition of competency-based educational programs is necessary. Throughout this volume, a competency is defined as "a combination of skills, abilities, and knowledge needed to perform a specific task" (U.S. Department of Education, 2001, p. 1). Competency-based learning models bundle competencies in ways that require students to demonstrate performance in a setting that more or less simulates the real-world context in which the competency would be applicable. Competency statements seek to reduce measurement to definable units that contain sufficient granularity as to be unequivocal. The definition of a competency statement as presented later in this volume by Alice Bedard Voorhees provides students and faculty

New Directions for Institutional Research, no. 110, Summer 2001 © John Wiley & Sons, Inc.

an unambiguous starting point. Ultimately, a competency statement should be written in such a way as to reflect the level of assessment necessary to demonstrate that learning has occurred.

Audience, Communication, and Purpose

Measuring or assessing competencies is not enough. For competency-based learning models to have real value, information about the quality and range of competencies needs to be available and communicated in meaningful, useful terms to a variety of audiences. There are two broad audiences for data and information about competency-based education. The first is an internal audience, including students, faculty, and staff. How can data and information about competencies be recorded and communicated so they are meaningful and useful for these different constituents? How can we tell students that they have achieved competencies in a way that permits them, in turn, to tell employers and others exactly what they can do? This is especially crucial when student transcripts continue to report traditional course titles and grades but not additional information about students' demonstrated knowledge and skills. How will faculty know that students have attained competencies in areas that transcend a particular course or discipline? How will advisers be able to advise students about areas where their competencies remain weak, or are of special strength?

The second broad audience is external to postsecondary institutions and includes state higher education agencies, accrediting organizations, and professional associations, as well as groups outside of education. Each of these constituencies can reasonably expect that competencies should be reported in clear, unambiguous terms. Employers, in particular, constitute an important segment of this external audience. Dennis Jones (2000) argues that students want certificates that have currency in the marketplace and provide documentation of competencies beyond a degree or list of courses completed. There is, however, an obvious economy at work here. Because brevity is valued, it is unlikely that employers will read through portfolios or multiple pages of information about a student's achievements. The challenge then is to construct summary data that are concise enough to satisfy employers while retaining sufficient richness to convey what the student has mastered.

The need to report meaningful student competencies is not a recent phenomenon. Lack of evidence of student competencies, coupled with employer and public perceptions about students' lack of preparation for either employment or further study, has fostered policies and practices such as accountability reporting, performance-based budgeting and funding, and learning-outcomes assessment for accreditation. Reporting meaningful competencies is not just an exercise but has the potential for reassuring external audiences about students' achievements. In the ideal world, this new reporting could address some of the external criticisms about lack of student preparation and the quality of postsecondary education. A clear under-standing of the motivations for engaging in competency-based learning models drives decisions about the appropriate and meaningful treatment of data and the information they generate.

It is especially important to determine whether competency assess-ments are intended to be formative, summative, or both. Formative assess-ments occur while a course or program is in progress. Data provide feedback to improve teaching and learning before the educational experience has ended. Summative assessments occur after a course or program is complete. They provide feedback about the totality of the experience after it has ended, but they are not useful for those seeking to modify and improve the experience while it is in progress. Neither approach is necessarily right or wrong, but the appropriate resolution of a host of data-related issues is con-tingent on which form of assessment is intended.

Considerations of audience, communication, and purpose form the touchstones to connect with the more specific data issues discussed later in the chapter. What good would it do, for example, to publish a scholarly article reporting student achievements of competencies in selected fields without telling the students themselves whether or not they have obtained the level of competency expected by employers in those fields? How would the scholarly article help students? Consider a different scenario. Department X develops an excellent competency-based education program through which students acquire knowledge, skills, and abilities that make them among the most sought-after recruits for key corporations. An impor-tant aspect of the program is that students receive immediate and concrete feedback about their competencies throughout the program, and employ-ers are given substantive information about student competencies that they recognize as valid descriptions of what students can really do. Students and employers know the worth of graduates, but others in the institution and at other colleges and universities are unaware of the program and struggle to give their students comparable competencies. How might information about this program assist other units and institutions to achieve similar results?

The lesson is simple. As institutions move to plan and implement com-petency-based educational programs, participants in the process should devote time and thought to specific definition of audience and purpose and then to the data issues inherent in competency-based education. Proper groundwork can save unintended downstream consequences. Every issue may not be solvable, but at least each issue should be considered, and a util-itarian, if not ideal, solution should be advanced for consideration.

Data Issues

After audience and purpose have been determined, it is important to con-sider several key data issues. These issues usually are played out at several levels in the institution.

Operational Definitions. The broad definition of a competency that was provided previously is generic but not directly useful for a specific learning module, course, or program. From the perspective of collecting, analyzing, interpreting, reporting, and using data about competencies, additional definitional attributes are important. The operational definitions of competencies need to be clear and meaningful to instructors, students, and target audiences. They must be aligned with the goals of the learning experience. This means that the course or major should be designed to result in the competencies identified. Finally, the competency, as defined, must be assessable. For many faculty members, the process of defining competencies to meet these characteristics is new, complicated, and time consuming, requiring new ways of thinking about their courses and instructional methodologies. Implicit is the need to involve students actively in course assignments that involve the integration of applied as well as theoretical contents.

Another issue associated with defining competencies is that definitions and measures of competency at one level should be consistent with and build on those used at other levels. This means that competency statements should be consistently written across courses and between years of study— that is, freshman, sophomore, junior, and senior years. This consistency also should extend across disciplines, across courses within a program, across general education courses, and across courses in the major. For example, the definition and measure of competency in verbal communication should be consistent across all these areas, although a higher degree of competency might be expected in advanced courses or within certain majors. Achieving this degree of consensus and consistency would require involvement of faculty across an institution, a demand quite different from more traditional definitions of knowledge, skills, and abilities that are constrained within a single department and may be quite different from definitions of similar competencies within another department.

Level at Which Competencies Are Defined and Assessed. Competencies can be assessed at a number of levels, such as an instructional unit within a course, a course, the major, or the institution as a whole. The acquisition of competencies can also be cumulative, building from modules to a complete course to a sequence of courses and even to the entire experience at an institution, including out-of-class as well as in-class experiences. Assessment of competencies at these levels invites many issues. First, the assessment instruments and processes need to be appropriate for the level at which competencies are defined and assessed. Second, the level should be relevant to the target audience; for example, if employers want graduates to be competent writers, they probably do not care whether academicians have equated their proficiency to the freshman or sophomore level. They are likely to care only about the finished product, the graduates' writing abilities. Third, the level should be relevant to the decision-making or policy development context that is being addressed. For example, if a department is assessing competency of its majors, then the level of most relevance would likely be key courses and arrays of courses within the major.

Unit of Analysis. Competencies can be assessed and results reported for individual students, cohorts of students, program (or major) graduates, and all graduates from a college within a university, or the institution as a whole. Two primary issues related to assessing competencies for various units are ensuring that assessment instruments and processes are appropriate and ensuring that the unit selected for analysis is relevant to the target audience. For example, if the target audience is the individual student, and assessment results are intended to give feedback to that student about his or her competencies, then obviously the individual student is the unit of analysis. A whole different approach can be appropriate for a target audience comprising external agencies such as accrediting bodies or state governing boards, where data from samples is typically acceptable for conveying information about achievements of students from a major or institution.

Assessment Data and Processes. Another set of considerations relates to the data and processes used to assess competencies. They need to be consistent with the goals of the learning experience—that is, designed to measure the desired outcomes of the course or major. They need to be clear and meaningful to the target audience. Assessment results should have utility for decisions such as improving teaching and learning, allocating resources, and informing consumers.

Measurement. Issues associated with measuring competencies are complex. Before discussing key issues, it is important to note the distinction between *applied* and *classical, or theoretical, research.* In brief, measuring competencies to assess learning and the extent to which students can *do* something is a process that takes place in settings that simulate the real world in which the task or set of tasks would be performed. Even if the physical setting is a classroom, the problem that students are asked to solve or the exercise that they are asked to perform is derived more or less from real situations. Classical or theoretical research, in contrast, pays strict attention to such attributes as research designs, creating control and treatment groups, and incorporating control variables into the analysis. These research approaches, labeled applied and classical (or theoretical), are not mutually exclusive. Rather, they describe two ends of a continuum. In the competency arena, it is unlikely that the measurement process can adhere to the strictest canons of social science research as presented in textbooks or demanded in traditional scholarly journals. At the same time, however, measuring competencies does require careful consideration of research issues and thoughtful procedures for incorporating sound research methodologies. Critics of competency-based educational initiatives may well find issues related to measurement as the most vulnerable point at which to launch an attack against the enterprise.

Reliability and validity are two key attributes of sound research. In the context of measuring competencies, reliability is the surety that a measurement technique, applied repeatedly across the same subjects, will yield the same results each time. Validity means that measurement reflects the true competency of the subject. For most constituencies facing validity, the belief that the measurement is reasonably related to the actual competency is the most important form of validity.

Validating Competencies. As a starting point for ensuring that competencies are valid in local circumstances, institutions can draw suitable competencies from existing compilations. The Internet has become a powerful tool for researching existing competencies, and specific models available there are reviewed in both Karen Paulson's and Alice Bedard Voorhees's chapters in this volume. Next, local companies or organizations interested in training are asked to validate the relevancy of these competency statements and to suggest their own. Similar processes are outlined by Erwin and Wise's chapter on establishing cutoff scores by using panels of experts.

Once concerns about validity are addressed, the remaining issues in measuring competencies include scoring rubrics. Here it is important that measurement scales and scoring metrics or rubrics used to measure competencies are clear and meaningful to instructors, students, and target audiences. It is important also that consistent metrics be used to assess different competencies; for example, applying different scales across several competencies could be misleading or confusing. Imagine a measurement scheme that used three-, five-, and seven-point scoring rubrics to assess competencies of graduates, with the highest number (three, five, or seven) always denoting the highest level of proficiency on that measure. Now consider the report of these assessments. Readers would have to keep straight whether a three was the top score on one set of measures, a middle-of-the-range score on another set, and a score denoting mediocre or even unacceptable proficiency on a third set.

Measurement issues extend beyond analyzing results of a specific instrument or rubric used to assess competency. External data such as the Law School Admissions Test or the Graduate Record Examination scores, performances in graduate school, and employer evaluations are examples of measures that can be used to validate competencies or to calibrate two or more competency measures. Precision, reliability, validity, credibility, and cost should all be considered in selecting locally developed versus externally or vendor-developed assessment tests and measures. Finally, there should be agreement on whether standards should be set to denote mastery or minimum acceptable competency.

Timeliness. Timeliness is yet another consideration in looking at data and information. There are two facets to timeliness. One deals directly with measurement and the other with currency of competencies. First, constructing, testing, revising, and authenticating the validity and reliability of measures can take a good deal of time, even years. This can also be costly. In fields where competencies change frequently, it is not unusual that by the time measures are subjected to rigorous tests of validity and reliability, the competencies assessed with those measures are no longer germane or important to that discipline or occupation—that is, the content of competencies has changed. Although this will not occur in broad areas such as teamwork, communication, writing, critical thinking, or mathematics, it certainly can occur in areas such as information technology or health professions. For the institution embarking on competency-based education, therefore, consideration must be given to balancing the cost and time required to create homegrown competency assessments with the possibility that the competencies measured will become outdated by the time the assessment is validated.

The second aspect of timeliness relates to whether the competencies were demonstrated within an appropriate time frame. This is analogous to a common postsecondary requirement that students can transfer courses in some subjects only if the courses were taken within a stipulated period of time, perhaps within the past five years, a stipulation intended to ensure the currency of students' knowledge. Imagine a person documenting competency in Wang word processing, and how useless that competency would be in today's labor market. This is an issue of both policy and practice. How recent should competencies be for the student to be eligible for course equivalency credit, for example? For how long should a postsecondary institution retain evidence such as portfolios that demonstrate a student has knowledge or skills that are simply outdated?

Data and Information Management

Issues of data and information management in competency-based learning models are sometimes not considered until institutions are well into the program. This set of issues may require conversations and support from offices outside the institutional research departments or direct education delivery units; consequently, they should be brought into the planning of competency-based learning models early on.

First, there should be a balance between the costs of obtaining, maintaining, analyzing, and reporting data about competencies on the one hand and the benefit or utility of data and information to target audiences on the other hand. Institutions might be dissuaded from absorbing the costs of reporting competencies when their existing systems of reporting more traditional measures, such as course grades or degrees, are well-known and perhaps culturally entrenched. The controlling decision might be the perception of the benefit or utility of data and information to target audiences.

Second, the institution has to decide how to store and maintain data and information relevant to assessing competencies, including records of workplace experiences and student portfolios. Institutions also need to decide whether data about student competencies should be incorporated in traditional transcripts, in innovative transcripts such as career transcripts, or in nontranscript databases. If the former, how will traditional transcripts and software applications need to be modified to accommodate the new elements? Whatever direction the institution pursues, data about competencies should be organized in ways that are most meaningful to target audiences—that is, mastery would be defined and documented at a level that makes ready sense to employers. Complex, multidimensional arrays of competencies should be avoided.

An alternative to the institution's retaining competency documentation, especially if the competency has been measured by a commercial or industry test, is for a testing agency, association within the industry, or commercial or not-for-profit corporation to act as a clearinghouse. Imagine an organization whose business is to record, store, and upon request disseminate a professional transcript containing not just traditional transcript data from postsecondary institutions but also verifications of licensure, certifications, and competencies demonstrated through recognized tests or on-the-job experiences. The company's customer would be the individual student, who would pay a fee for the service. Obviously, there would have to be protocols and guarantees that competencies and experiences included in the student's record were bona fide and validated so that recipients of the professional transcript would have confidence in its accuracy. Such a transcript is analogous in some ways to one's financial history as reported by credit bureaus that provide a history of one's credit transactions regardless of the company with which they took place.

Portability. As competency-based learning models grow, portability of competencies across institutions will become more significant. First, definitions of competency and assessment procedures should be accepted across relevant organizational units and jurisdictions, such as secondary schools and colleges and universities. This might lead to meaningful comparisons of competencies between different levels of education—for example, secondary schools, undergraduate education, graduate schools. Pressures to make education seamless between secondary, undergraduate, and graduate education have fostered pressure to offer dual high school–college credit for certain courses and to expand the ways in which students can obtain college credit for work completed at the high school. Assessing competencies agreed to by both levels could be a viable alternative to comparing course contents and assignments and could ensure course equivalency.

Competency measures should be translatable by the receiving institution into traditional metrics of student progress, such as courses passed and credits earned. The proliferation of vendor-based certifications in certain fields—for example, Novell and Microsoft certifications—makes this a current and not just a theoretical issue at many institutions. Course equivalency credits, course waivers, and other representations of academic progress awarded through competency assessments need to be honored by other departments or schools within a university and by other institutions when a student transfers. Admissions offices at undergraduate and graduate schools should use student demonstrations or verifications of competency other than through traditional course credits. The task in this regard would be to ensure that competencies are reported using language and certifications recognized within an industry or occupation as well as within the postsecondary education community.

Reporting. Documented student competencies may be of interest to diverse audiences, each of which has its own tradition and framework for reporting data and information. Within postsecondary education, audiences are very familiar with traditional transcripts but less accustomed to narrative transcripts, portfolios, or other means of reporting students' achievements. Outside of postsecondary education, there is some question as to whether employers look at transcripts anyway or have the patience and understanding to read long reports of students' accomplishments. In some fields, there are very detailed skills standards for individuals seeking entry to selected occupations. These standards could provide a template for reporting students' achievements. It is not clear whether employers actually employ skills standards to screen potential employees or make decisions about promoting current employees. Attempts to craft reporting formats that align with skills standards may therefore have little actual utility.

As postsecondary institutions develop formats and mechanisms for reporting competencies, they might consider talking with key audiences for these reports to learn from them what they would find most useful. Usefulness includes not only the content of data and information but also the format used to convey them.

Examples of Documenting Competencies

Despite the importance of addressing and resolving data issues in competency-based education, including how to document competencies, it seems that few postsecondary institutions have dealt with these issues in any comprehensive, organized fashion. Wilson, Miles, Baker, and Schoenberger (2000) report, for example, that community college activity in documenting twenty-first-century skills in ways other than grades and course credit is well below the level of activity reported in defining, integrating, teaching, and assessing these skills. In their survey of 259 community colleges, only 5 percent reported full implementation of alternate forms of documentation. Another 34 percent said they have achieved partial implementation, although there was little information about what forms that documentation might take. Examples of documenting competencies at the institutional level follow.

Electronic Portfolios. In fall 1997, the University of Wisconsin-Superior (UWS) began a pilot project to develop a portfolio program for assessing its general education program. Students create and maintain two types of portfolios, the developmental and the showcase portfolio. The developmental portfolio contains examples of a student's work from early drafts to finished products. The showcase portfolio contains a variety of materials, all of which are intended to reflect the student's best work. For example, a showcase portfolio might include interactive résumés, documents submitted to support graduate school admission applications, and letters from internship supervisors. UWS now is beginning to address the issue of evaluating portfolios; faculty in each discipline will define criteria for assessing students' work.

Rose-Hulman Institute developed its electronic portfolio, entitled the RosE-Portfolio (Katz and Gangnon, 2000). Students are provided a template and interactive software that permits them to customize their portfolio to illustrate a variety of knowledge and skills. Hotlinks embedded in the portfolio can take the reader to other examples of the student's work. These portfolios are also developmental in nature. Faculty have access to rate portfolios and advisers have access to review a student's progress. These examples suggest how portfolios can be used to document competencies with concrete examples of student work. Portfolios have utility for students, as they can see the connections between learning experiences and prospective employers. At the same time, issues such as verifying that work submitted was really completed by the student and evaluating the quality of work are but two examples of the complexities raised by using portfolios to document competencies (see Rogers and Chow, 2000, for more information).

Experiential Learning. Since 1972, the School for New Learning (SNL) of De Paul University has provided a competency-based, highly individualized liberal arts undergraduate education designed for working adults. This concept has been extended since the 1980s, when graduate programs at the master's level were introduced. Students can earn degrees in SNL's largest program, the bachelor's in liberal arts, by fulfilling fifty competencies that are divided among five areas: lifelong learning (the core of transferable skills), the human community (social sciences), arts and ideas (humanities), the scientific world (natural sciences), and the individual focus area (the student's concentration). Twelve lifelong-learning competencies and one competency in each of the three liberal-learning areas (human community, arts and ideas, and the scientific world) are required. Students demonstrate and are assessed on their competencies in several ways. They can take specially designed SNL courses, complete student-designed individual learning pursuits, pass appropriate examinations, or document that transfer courses meet competencies. All assessments are done based on competency statements, which are further specified in related criteria and narrative examples.

Assessment at SNL occurs throughout the curriculum and often involves multiple assessors, including the student. The first lifelong-learning course, known as the "learning assessment seminar," involves self-assessment and diagnostic and placement exercises, which are assessed initially by academic advisers. When students enroll in SNL, they are assigned a faculty mentor with whom they will work until graduation. The faculty mentor is the initial assessor of transfer course work and independent learning. The school's faculty assessment committee provides a second review. Once students have identified a concentration, the focus area, a professional adviser from a relevant field joins the faculty mentor to guide and assess the students' overall learning plans and their specific focus area competencies. Faculty assess competencies earned through SNL courses. SNL has created its own instruments to assess competency in writing, quantitative skills, and critical thinking for those students who wish to fulfill those competencies through examination.

Assessment at the School for New Learning links teaching, advising, and evaluating with learning, thus providing feedback and guidance to learners, faculty, and the school. Explicit statements of assumptions, qualities for effective assessment, and guidelines for good practice inform SNL's assessment practices, which were developed and formally adopted by the faculty. The core qualities of effective assessment at SNL are clarity, integrity, flexibility, empathy, and efficiency. In 1998, in response to a faculty initiative, SNL created an assessment center to support and advance assessing in the service of adult learning. The undergraduate program is moving toward a learning-portfolio approach. At present, however, earned competencies are documented in traditional transcripts by letter-number designators such as L-1, which refers to the first competency in the lifelong-learning category, and in narrative transcripts in which the complete competency statements appear (Thomas A. Angelo, personal communication with author about De Paul University School of New Learning, July 31, 2000).

Conclusion

The data implications of competency-based educational programs can be daunting. Certainly, they are more complex and novel than the data implications of traditional postsecondary education programs. This chapter has attempted to spell out a number of these implications and to urge institutions to take these into account as they pursue competency-based learning models.

References

Jones, D. "From the President." *National Center for Higher Education Management News,* June 2000, *16,* 1–7.

Katz, A. M., and Gangnon, B. A. "Portfolio Assessment: Integrating Goals and Objectives with Learner Outcomes." *Assessment Update,* 2000, *12*(1), 6–7, 13.

Rogers, G. M., and Chow, T. "Electronic Portfolios and the Assessment of Student Learning." *Assessment Update,* 2000, *12*(1), 4–5, 11–12.

U.S. Department of Education, National Center for Education Statistics. *Defining and Assessing Learning: Exploring Competency-Based Initiatives* (by E. Jones, R. A. Voorhees, and K. Paulson for the Council of the National Postsecondary Education Cooperative

Competency-Based Initiatives Working Group). Washington, D.C.: U.S. Department of Education, National Center for Education Statistics, 2001.

Wilson, C. D., Miles, C. L., Baker, R. L., and Schoenberger, R. L. *Learning Outcomes for the 21st Century: Report of a Community College Study*. Mission Viejo, Calif.: League for Innovation in the Community College and The Pew Charitable Trusts, 2000.

TRUDY H. BERS is senior director of research, curriculum, and planning at Oakton Community College, Des Plaines, Illinois.

4

Competencies can play a critical role in institutional viability, especially as institutions link them to skills needed in today's workplace. Familiarity with what employers require of graduates will be an increasingly important intelligence for institutional researchers in the foreseeable future.

Using Competencies to Connect the Workplace and Postsecondary Education

Karen Paulson

Postsecondary education has become progressively responsive to the needs of business and industry, where learning is closely tied to competencies and performance-based assessment of those competencies. Critics condemn this accelerating trend in postsecondary education as evidence that institutions are moving away from their obligation to provide liberal education and toward mere credentialing. In contrast, advocates note that competencies are the underpinnings of traditional courses and degrees. This chapter highlights the use of competencies in business, discusses skill levels in the workforce, and then summarizes available skill and competency resources that can be used by institutions to prepare graduates to successfully enter today's performance-driven labor market.

Changes Occurring in Both Education and Business

Competencies have become more prevalent in K–12 and postsecondary education, partially because institutions have attempted to be more responsive to business needs (Ennis, 1998; Resnick and Wirt, 1996; Task Force on High-Performance Work and Workers, 1995, 1997; Zemsky and Cappelli, 1998). This movement is predated by widespread interest within the business sector, especially among corporate trainers, who routinely use competencies as a unit of analysis (Fuller and Farrington, 1999; Lucia and Lepsinger, 1999; Robinson and Robinson, 1999). This shift underlies the gradual movement toward performance-based models in the human resources field. Paralleling the move in postsecondary education toward

New Directions for Institutional Research, no. 110, Summer 2001 © John Wiley & Sons, Inc.

competencies and a corresponding focus on learning outcomes rather than on mere "seat time," training in business is also shifting from imparting skills to emphasizing results. The "focus is on what people need to do with what they learn, not on the acquisition of skill or knowledge. Training is seen as a means to the ultimate goal of enhancing performance" (Robinson and Robinson, 1999, p. 242). Whether the relationship between business and higher education will ever be a more symbiotic collaboration is debatable. Even so, it seems obvious that educators can no longer rely on mere convening of classes and granting of diplomas as sufficient proof that their graduates meet workplace needs. The common ground between higher education and business can be strengthened by the use of competencies in three primary areas: hiring, training, and promotion.

In the technologically and structurally expanding workplace, employers increasingly view diplomas and degrees with skepticism and want different measures to use when recruiting and retraining employees. Competencies can offer a suitable alternative. In the hiring process, some firms seek to "buy" skills up front, in lieu of "making" the skills later via in-house training (Zemsky and others, 1998). Buying the necessary skills appeals to some corporations because it is perceived as simpler and more cost-effective than anticipating the rapidly changing workplace and training employees for future skills. There appears to exist a large gap between the types of jobs available and the skills possessed by prospective employees. The 1997 National Employer Survey reports that attitude is the most desirable characteristic that employers seek in prospective employees, followed closely by ability to communicate. The next several characteristics, in decreasing order, are previous job performance, full-time work experience, industry-based credential, education level, after-school or summer work, and technical course work. Each of these characteristics is more closely associated with other jobs (formal, summer, or after school), education, or some credentialing process than with the formal education offered by most traditional institutions of higher education. Those characteristics rated as having little or no influence on employment decisions included pure academics, what someone does in her or his spare time, and high school reputation (Zemsky and others, 1998).

Companies are of three types in the hiring process. In the extremes, some companies assume that new hires already have the skills needed to perform the work for which they are employed; other companies believe that it is an employee's exclusive responsibility to redress competency gaps (National Workforce Assistance Collaborative, 1995). Companies that believe it is their responsibility to provide basic education to their employees occupy the middle ground. Where a company falls on this continuum determines the extent to which and what kind of training they offer their employees. Maintaining full training units may not be cost-effective for smaller companies nor productive for larger companies. Some corporations are moving away from maintaining in-house training departments and toward outsourcing their training needs, either to corporate universities or to postsecondary institutions (Robinson and Robinson, 1999). Competency statements become a useful common language, helping corporations and these units work together, because they describe exact behaviors and actions that will result from training, allowing for a better shared understanding of what is required from an employee than might be possible with less precise goals. This emphasis on competency statements will likely increase in the future. What occupations will businesses need to fill? And what competencies and skills will these occupations require?

Future Workforce

By 2006, the overall occupational complexion of the nation will change. Projections indicate an increase in the service industry, especially in the professional specialty industry, which includes occupations such as teachers and librarians and computer, math, and operations research personnel. Similarly, growth in technician and related support occupations will occur almost completely within the service industry, particularly in health, engineering, and management sectors. Some occupations, including computer operators, accountants, and secretaries, will decrease as automation increases. High growth will occur among other occupations that involve a great deal of contact with people, such as investigators, hotel desk clerks, receptionists, and information clerks (Silvestri, 1997).

Even given the previous comments in this chapter about the relatively low priority placed on pure academics by employers, the connection between education levels and employment is not likely to disappear anytime soon. Some level of formal education always will be required. For example, according to the U.S. Department of Labor, five of the six fastest-growing occupations require at least a bachelor's degree, and the sixth requires an associate degree (Bureau of Labor Statistics, 1999). Despite the currency of a bachelor's degree for landing one of the fastest-growing occupations, over 65 percent of the projected overall growth rate will be in occupations that do not require a bachelor's degree, although these jobs are lower paying and have poor benefits (Bureau of Labor Statistics, 1999). Finally, although jobs will be available for low- or no-skill workers, those jobs will provide much lower wages, far below a "living wage." Clearly, education will be key to employment in many occupations in the twenty-first century, although the credentialing function will increasingly be shaped by competencies.

Literacy and Competency Levels in the Workforce

Why the concern about the skills necessary for participation in the twenty-first-century workforce? At the turn of the new century, the economy is strong, unemployment is low, and the workforce is growing. These signs belie a new reality, however. A new form of unemployment is developing, one characterized by a surplus of people who lack the competencies necessary to fill available jobs (Immerwahr, Johnson, and Kernan-Schloss, 1991). Empirical evidence indicates that corporations employing or cultivating highly educated workforces have correspondingly higher productivity levels. Employees who are given formal training enjoy an average increase in productivity of between 15 and 20 percent. These benefits extend to employers as well. The federal government reports that companies that employ a workforce whose educational attainment level was 10 percent higher than other, related companies enjoyed an 8.6 percent greater average productivity. Contrast these gains with a 3.4 percent productivity gain resulting from a 10 percent increase in average capital investment (U.S. Department of Commerce and others, 1999). For individuals, each additional year of schooling beyond the high school degree increases annual earnings 8 to 9 percent (National Alliance of Business, 1996). Beyond economics, the connection between education and individual well-being is yet another advantage of increasing employee performance. Small and midsized companies that engaged in raising employee levels of basic workplace skills experienced subsequent increases in worker "motivation, self-esteem, willingness to take responsibility, teamwork, and communication and problem solving abilities" (National Workforce Assistance Collaborative, 1995, p. 2).

An often overlooked but critical area of competency desired by employers is literacy. The National Adult Literacy Survey (NALS) defines literacy as "using printed and written information to function in society, to achieve one's goals, and to develop one's knowledge and potential" (Barton, 1999, p. 6). NALS assesses three types of literacy—prose literacy, document literacy, and quantitative literacy. Scores for each type are divided into five levels representing low to high literacy levels: Level 1 = 0–225; Level 2 = 226–275; Level 3 = 276–325; Level 4 = 326–375; and Level 5 = 376–500. Results from the NALS are disturbing. Seventy percent of the unemployed persons taking the assessment scored in the lowest two categories of prose literacy, and only 5 percent were in the top two categories (U.S. Department of Commerce and others, 1999). Low levels of prose literacy among the unemployed not only impede the advancement and functioning in the labor force of these individuals but also affect collectively that of the entire United States economy. Additional results from the NALS indicate that 65 percent of unemployed adults are unable to interpret uncomplicated tables, graphs, and maps. The problems of literacy are not exclusively those of the unemployed, however. More than 20 percent of Americans possess literacy and numeracy skills at or below the fifth-grade level. An additional 25 to 28 percent of individuals test slightly higher, between the sixth- and eighth-grade levels. Finally, data indicate that the United States has a greater proportion of adults with low skills than any of the other nations in the Organization for Economic Cooperation and Development (U.S. Department of Commerce and others, 1999).

Barton (1999) researched the interrelationship between literacy and occupations, starting with 1986 data and projecting to 2006. The twenty-five fastest-growing occupations defined by percentage increase required higher levels of literacy (308) than that present in the overall employed population (291). In contrast, literacy levels for the twenty-five occupations with the largest proportional decreases averaged 291. A similar analysis of the twenty-five largest-increasing occupations defined numerically revealed a mix of high and low literacy requirements. Over time, average literacy levels have remained stable among the employed (Barton, 1999). Despite this stability, there is a considerable gap between occupations. The average score for the twenty-five occupations with the highest prose literacy requirements was 345, whereas the average score for the twenty-five occupations with the lowest prose literacy requirements was 246.

Barton points out that although literacy level is not a proxy for education level, it is often related to the number of years of education. Even so, literacy scores are dispersed broadly (approximately from 230 to 340) at each education level. Several reasons are given to explain this phenomenon. There is a connection between educational achievement and the individual that can be explained, in part, by "the quality of the institution a student attended. Also, the literacy assessment measures proficiency in performing day-to-day real-world tasks, not proficiency with subject-matter material taught in schools" (Barton, 1999, p. 20–21). The education-literacy gap also can be traced to the differences in individual abilities across subject matter. For instance, the skills needed to complete an English major compared with those of a statistics major can lead to different literacy levels. Ultimately, earnings are directly related to literacy level within each education level— that is, individuals with higher literacy scores earn more money than their peers with the same education. Weekly wages for a four-year college graduate increase with literacy level: Level 1 = \$357, Level 2 = \$466, Level 3 = \$503, Level 4 = \$561, and Level 5 = \$631. Similarly, average weekly wages for two-year graduates increase like this: Level 1 = \$335, Level 2 = \$408, Level 3 = \$407, Level 4 = \$460, and Level 5 = \$532 (Barton, 1999, p. 21). Such data are further evidence of the importance not only of education level but also of assessing competency in the hiring process.

The incidence of low basic workplace skills among today's workers in the United States ranges from 20 percent to as high as 40 percent of the workforce (National Workforce Assistance Collaborative, 1995). Further, 40 percent of manufacturing executives believe that their companies are unable to "upgrade technologically" because of the low literacy and basic skills of their workers. Thirty percent believe that low skills also affect their abilities to improve productivity, and another 30 percent stated that reorganization was impossible because employees were incapable of learning new tasks (National Association of Manufacturers study cited in National Workforce Assistance Collaborative, 1995). The 1995 National Employer Survey found that respondents thought that only 80 percent of their employees were "proficient at their jobs." Of surveyed employers, 32 percent thought that 75 percent or fewer of their employees were proficient, and only 19 percent believed that almost all of their employees (over 95 percent) were proficient at what they were hired to do (National Workforce Assistance Collaborative, 1995).

These bleak appraisals appear to cut across job titles. Thirty percent of companies responding to a recent survey by the Center for Public Resources thought that their secretaries were unable to read at a level high enough to complete their job assignments. Managers and supervisors at 50 percent of the companies were reported to have trouble producing grammatically correct paragraphs. Half of the companies reported that their skilled and semiskilled employees were unable to correctly use fractions and decimals (National Workforce Assistance Collaborative, 1995). In the 1994 National Employer Survey, 56 percent of companies replied that the skills necessary for fulfilling jobs in their companies were increasing, and only 5 percent noted a decrease in required skill levels (Saul, 1998). Statistics and findings such as these are not encouraging given the needs of twenty-first-century workplaces. Indeed, in a recent *Time* article, Tom Peters (2000) hypothesized that "90% of white-collar jobs in the U.S. will be either destroyed or altered beyond recognition in the next 10 to 15 years" (p. 68). Basic skills and competencies are necessary because they allow people to be nimble and change areas of focus on the job. Given this low baseline, what can and should postsecondary institutions do to help? They can begin by examining the basic skills and competencies necessary for successful employment in the twenty-first-century economy.

Basic Skills and Competencies
Linking Education and Business

Many blue-ribbon panels and commissions have collected and published the skills and competencies necessary for success in today's economy and occupations. Often these compilations include desired workplace attitudes in addition to the knowledge and performance-based competencies that prospective employees should have. This section begins with an overview of these collections. Later, these skills are summarized into a single integrated list.

SCANS Skills and Career Transcripts. The Secretary's Commission on Achieving Necessary Skills (SCANS) is a large-scale federal program designed to name key employment skills (see www.scans.jhu.edu). In 1991, SCANS first published three foundation skills areas: basic skills (reading, writing, arithmetic and mathematics, speaking, and listening), thinking skills (thinking creatively, making decisions, solving problems, seeing things in the mind's eye, knowing how to learn, and reasoning), and personal qualities (such as developing individual responsibility, self-esteem, sociability, self-management, and integrity). SCANS further elaborated the competencies that workers should be able to do "productively." First, they must be able to use resources in terms of allocating time, money, materials, space, and staff. Second, employees should use interpersonal skills when working in teams, teaching others, serving customers, and leading, negotiating, and working with people. Third, productive personnel use information by acquiring and evaluating data, organizing and maintaining files, interpreting and communicating, and using computers to process information. Fourth, individuals must be able to use systems, including understanding social, organizational, and technological systems, monitoring and correcting performance, and designing or improving systems. Finally, employees must be able to use technology when selecting equipment and tools, applying technology to specific tasks, and maintaining and troubleshooting technologies.

SCANS also has been used to document competency in the same way that traditional transcripts issued by higher education institutions document credit hours. Particularly useful for the entry-level graduate, the *career transcript* that SCANS 2000 promotes can document broader language and math proficiencies as well as desirable workplace characteristics and attitudes. Institutions that assess these competencies by using SCANS and other workplace assessments provide graduates with formal documentation that has currency in industry circles.

Other researchers also have examined the skills needed in the workplace. In contrast to SCANS, these compilations generally operate at a broader level.

The Bases of Competence. Evers, Rush, and Berdrow (1998) have extracted four *base competencies* that all workers should have. These are managing self—that is, "constantly developing practices and internalizing routines for maximizing one's ability to deal with the uncertainty of an ever-changing environment"; communicating, which is described as effective interaction that uses both verbal and written methods to deliver and receive information; managing people and tasks—in other words, "accomplishing the tasks at hand by planning, organizing, coordinating, and controlling both resources and people"; and mobilizing innovation and change, which is described as "conceptualizing, as well as setting in motion, ways of initiating and managing change that involve significant departures from the current mode" (p. 5).

The New Basic Skills. Murnane and Levy (1996) identified *new basic skills* that they believe students should master by the end of high school and before attending college—skills critical to obtaining a middle-class job in today's economy. They include these personal characteristics: reliability, a positive attitude, and a willingness to work hard. Desirable *hard skills* are "basic mathematics, problem-solving and reading abilities at levels much higher than many high school graduates now attain (p. 9)." Necessary *soft skills* include "the ability to work in groups and to make effective oral and written presentations—skills many schools do not teach (p. 9)." Finally, Murnane and

Levy acknowledge the need to be able to use a personal computer to complete simple tasks. Ability levels are referenced to what should be required of ninth graders, including ninth-grade-level math and reading, the ability to solve semistructured problems using hypothesis testing, the ability to work with individuals from varying places, and the ability to communicate effectively in writing and in person.

Twenty-First-Century Skills for Twenty-First-Century Jobs. The document *21st Century Skills for 21st Century Jobs* from the federal government summarizes desirable workplace skills, with heavy emphasis on basic cognitive skills, including reading, writing, and computation. They recommend minimum employee reading skills that include the ability to read safety postings and, at a slightly higher level, instructions and forms. This report found that the need for organizational skills is increasing in importance as new styles of management predominate in the workplace. Here, communication skills, analytical skills, problem solving and creative thinking, interpersonal skills, the ability to negotiate and influence, and self-management become paramount (U.S. Department of Commerce and others, 1999). On the technical side, the need for computer skills is highlighted as a basic requirement because computers are now used not only to increase productivity but also to enhance customer delivery and interaction.

Computer use is increasing at an amazing rate. In 1984, only 26 percent of the workforce used computers on the job; by 1993, it had increased to 48 percent. Business spending on information technology in 1986 represented 25 percent of total business equipment investment. Ten years later, information technology's share had risen 20 percentage points to 45 percent. For industries such as communications, insurance, and investment brokerages, information technology constitutes over three-quarters of all equipment investments. And over 40 percent of production and nonsupervisory employees in manufacturing and service establishments use computers (U.S. Department of Commerce and others, 1999). All workers will need to be computer savvy, because a high-performance, high-productivity, and high-wage economy is entwined with advances in information technology.

Carnevale (1996) emphasizes the need to return to the basics of reading, writing, and arithmetic—with a twist. He argues that the emphasis must be on how to apply these basic skills. He also believes that employees have trouble seeing how they fit into the larger picture either intellectually or in a business sense, "The key skill . . . is the ability of every worker to take responsibility for the final product or service, irrespective of their particular job assignment" (Carnevale, 1996, pp. 9–10).

What Business Wants from Higher Education. In *What Business Wants from Higher Education*, Oblinger and Verville (1998) have synthesized corporate research studies of the skills required of bachelor's degree recipients. They include many of the other skills that have been discussed here; however, they include an in-depth analysis of problem solving as a skill. Problem solving and making decisions is disaggregated into six steps. The first step is to be able to recognize a problem as a problem. Second, individuals must be able to accurately define the parameters of the problem. The third step is to formulate several strategies to solve the problem. The next two steps are accurately presenting the information used to solve the problem and explaining how resources need to be allocated to achieve the proposed solution. The last step is monitoring and evaluating the outcome of the proposed solution. A decision is made when, based on the various steps, a particular solution is chosen for implementation and a rationale for that solution can be presented.

The implications of a global economy also spill over into skill compilations. Skills in globalism and multicultural competence are critical to America's ability to compete internationally. *Globalism* means knowing how to operate differently because of understanding international systems in general and their meaning in a particular area for the business at hand, whereas *multicultural competence* is defined as "an internationalized understanding plus the attitudes, skills, and domain knowledge needed to apply it effectively in a specific context" (Bikson, 1996, p. 14–15). Bikson explains that a person with multicultural competence understands how the various parts of the world "govern themselves" as well as how nations interact, is open to new cultures, and has foreign language fluency.

An often-overlooked skill that is desired by business is worth a final mention in this section dealing with skill compilations. Namely, business leaders want employees with a modest level of business acumen (Task Force on High-Performance Work and Workers, 1995, 1997). This means that employees should understand the "role of the corporation," basic budgets, and resource allocation. They note that college "graduates are not prepared for the competitive demands of today's leaner, flatter corporation, its relentless preoccupation with quality and customer needs, and the rate at which it is changing" (1995, p. 11).

Summary. Exhibit 4.1 synthesizes the workplace skills presented in this chapter.

To clearly differentiate the "types" of skills, they are arranged in Exhibit 4.1 in four categories—attitudes and personal characteristics, essential skills, integrative-applied skills, and premium skills. The labels for these categories were chosen for specific reasons. First, the use of "basic" with respect to skills has become hackneyed, and there is a wide range of meanings in use. Perspectives on the proper meaning for the term *basic skills* range from those who believe that only "essential skills" are basic to those who believe that all the skills listed in Exhibit 4.1 are basic, in the sense that they are crucial to effective participation in today's labor market. Still others will select different skill levels from across one or more categories to arrive at basic skills. Each perspective is correct in its own way, based on the context from which the issue is viewed. Exhibit 4.1 relies on the term *essential* as the elemental level of skill required from everyone in the workplace. Almost all of these skills for the twenty-first century—especially essential

Exhibit 4.1. Summary of Twenty-First-Century Workplace Skills

Attitudes and Personal Characteristics

Adaptability, flexibility, resiliency, ability to accept ambiguity
Common sense and ability to anticipate downstream consequences
Creativity
Empathy
Positive attitude, good work ethic, ability to self-manage
Reliability, dependability
Responsibility, honesty, integrity

Essential Skills

Computer skills for simple tasks (word processing)
Interpersonal skills, team skills
Numeracy and computation skills at a ninth-grade level, including basic money skills
Reading at a ninth-grade level
Speaking and listening
Writing

Integrative-Applied Skills

Application of technology to tasks
Critical thinking
Customer contact skills
Information use skills
Presentation skills
Problem recognition–definition–solution formulation
Reasoning

Premium Skills

Ability to understand organizational and contextual issues (legal, environmental)
Basic resource management, ability to work with budgets
Ethics
Foreign language fluency
Globalism, internationalism skills
Multicultural-competence skills
Negotiation skills
Project management and supervision
Systems thinking

skills—are also generic skills, a structure necessary to accommodate the half-life of domain-specific knowledge. Information becomes quickly obsolete in today's economy; therefore, it is critical that potential employees be broadly competent so that they can continue to learn and develop new skills and knowledge. The "integrative-applied" category reflects the reality that many of the essential skills in Exhibit 4.1 require application in more complex situations. For example, "presentation skills" are an application of essential speaking and listening skills. Finally, rather than calling "advanced" skills just that, "premium" was used. This decision was made for two reasons. First, whereas both integrative-applied and premium skills are desirable, essential skills are mandatory. Second, many premium skills are found in potential employees who are not traditionally considered advanced. For example, there are many individuals for whom English is a second or third language; they likely already have two of the premium skills, multicultural competence and foreign language fluency, even though they may typically not be considered advanced.

These are the competencies that are required for employment at a living wage in the twenty-first-century economy. For postsecondary graduates to be prepared at a minimum to enter the workforce, they must possess these essential skills. Being competent at both integrative-applied and premium skills soon may be expected of bachelor's degree recipients. Finally, in any form of employment, certain attitudinal and personal characteristics are desirable.

Linking Postsecondary Education and Business

Opponents' fearing vocationalism aside, postsecondary education institutions must reach a working relationship with business and industry to create educated competent workers for the twenty-first-century workforce. The result must be a partnership; many business leaders have been quite clear that they do not wish to dictate to faculty and administrators how to best create competent graduates. But the goal remains to achieve the best scenario for individuals, businesses, and academic institutions, resulting in learned and competent graduates. In addition, corporations are hoping to be able to partner with postsecondary institutions for their training needs. The competencies and skills listed in Exhibit 4.1 are a useful starting point for forming these partnerships.

In fact, most of the competencies included in Exhibit 4.1 are the result of the liberal arts or the general education component of the curriculum. They are not traditional outcomes of vocational or technical subjects. Degree titles tend to indicate competence in the major, particularly at the cognitive or knowledge level, not at the application or "doing" level. The reality of needing specific knowledge areas leads many businesses to use degree attainment as a proxy for competency in the hiring process. But stories are rampant of, for example, brilliant engineering graduates from all types of institutions who are incapable of applying and doing anything with their book knowledge. What needs to happen in postsecondary institutions is that the specific competencies—like those listed in Exhibit 4.1—need to be explicitly discussed and analyzed for their inclusion in all curricula. In addition, students themselves need to be taught how to recognize these competencies as outcomes of their education.

Current students and new graduates must highlight their competencies when applying for jobs. These methods are especially crucial because traditional grades and standardized tests often do not measure competence, so people with potential to be excellent employees are culled out of the interview process because of low scores on traditional measures. Suggestions for overcoming this obstacle include describing key competencies for the particular job in the cover letter and on the first page of the résumé, along with specific instances of when and how the competency was developed. For instance, an engineering student might list "teamwork skills" directly under degree information on the résumé, along with a short description of an Engineering 101 class in which the student's three-person team rotated leadership and follower roles while building a structure. Some recruiters and human resource personnel have started using qualitative-research software to scan cover letters and résumés for key words and phrases, many of which are found in the list of skills and competencies. Students also should be prepared in interviews to talk about specific instances when they demonstrated key attitudes and characteristics. A resource for students who are seeking entry to the workplace may be the career transcript, which captures skills and not courses for presentation to employers. Students and new graduates should be exposed in classes or through career placement services' workshops to the assessment methods used by businesses, including skills tests, realistic job previews, job simulations, and assessment centers (Bassi, 1999). They should also be taught how to focus on the competencies that were learned as part of the general education part of the curriculum.

Conclusion

The increasing use of competencies creates several opportunities for institutional researchers. First, it is an opportunity to rethink tracking and academic management information systems in terms of competencies. This requires eliminating most time-based definitions and categorizations found among data elements; it calls for new file structures that incorporate competency assessment scores, including dates when performance assessments were taken and retaken. It also creates the possibility of expanding (or instituting) existing alumni surveys to track students and graduates into the workplace using unemployment insurance wage records and other state agency data. Another area that is not currently focused on to any extent by institutional researchers is that of employer needs assessments. These assessments are useful in determining what certifications and degree programs might be most beneficial for the surrounding economic region.

In order for postsecondary graduates to be employed in the twenty-first-century workforce, certain skills and competencies will be needed. A partnership of postsecondary education paired with business can work to expose individuals to these competencies and their importance. This chapter focused on the use of competencies in business, how certain competencies are critical to a vibrant American workforce, what basic skills and competencies are necessary for employment in the twenty-first century, and how postsecondary education and business can work together to strengthen these competencies among postsecondary graduates and employees.

References

Barton, P. E. *What Jobs Require: Literacy, Education, and Training, 1940–2006.* Princeton, N.J.: Educational Testing Service, 1999.

Bassi, L. J. "Are Employers' Recruitment Strategies Changing: Competence Over Credentials?" In N. G. Stacey (ed.), *Competence Without Credentials.* Washington, D.C.: U.S. Department of Education, Mar. 1999. [www.ed.gov/pubs/Competence/section3.html].

Bikson, T. K. "Educating a Globally Prepared Workforce: New Research on College and Corporate Perspectives." *Liberal Education,* 1996, *82*(2), 12–19.

Bureau of Labor Statistics. "Tomorrow's Jobs." *1998–99 Occupational Outlook Handbook.* Washington, D.C.: Bureau of Labor Statistics, 1999. [stats.bls.gov/oco/oco2003.htm].

Carnevale, A. P. "Liberal Education and the New Economy." *Liberal Education,* 1996, 82(2), 4–11.

Ennis, S. "Assessing Employee Competencies." In S. M. Brown and C. J. Seidner (eds.), *Evaluating Corporate Training: Models and Issues.* Norwell, Mass.: Kluwer, 1998.

Evers, F. T., Rush, J. C., and Berdrow, I. *The Bases of Competence: Skills for Lifelong Learning and Employability.* San Francisco: Jossey-Bass, 1998.

Fuller, J., and Farrington, J. *From Training to Performance Improvement: Navigating the Transition.* San Francisco: Jossey-Bass, 1999.

Immerwahr, J., Johnson, J., and Kernan-Schloss, A. *Cross Talk: The Public, the Experts, and Competitiveness.* Research report. Washington, D.C.: Business–Higher Education Forum and Public Agenda Foundation, Feb. 1991.

Lucia, A. D., and Lepsinger, R. *The Art and Science of Competency Models: Pinpointing Critical Success Factors in Organizations.* San Francisco: Jossey-Bass, 1999.

Murnane, R. J., and Levy, F. *Teaching the New Basic Skills: Principles for Educating Children to Thrive in a Changing Economy.* New York: Free Press, 1996.

National Alliance of Business. *The Impact of Workforce Quality in the New American Economy.* Washington, D.C.: National Alliance of Business, 1996.

National Workforce Assistance Collaborative. *Basic Workplace Skills: The Foundation of Productivity Improvement.* Workforce Brief no. 4. Washington, D.C.: National Alliance of Business, 1995.

Oblinger, D. G., and Verville, A. L. *What Business Wants from Higher Education.* Phoenix: Oryx Press, 1998.

Peters, T. "What Will We Do for Work?" *Time,* May 22, 2000, pp. 68–71.

Resnick, L. B., and Wirt, J. G. (eds.). *Linking School and Work: Roles for Standards and Assessment.* San Francisco: Jossey-Bass, 1996.

Robinson, D. G., and Robinson, J. C. "The Shift from Training to Performance." In *The 1999 Annual: Volume 1 (Training).* San Francisco: Jossey-Bass/Pfeiffer, 1999.

Saul, R. S. "On Connecting School and Work." *Annals of the American Academy of Political and Social Science,* Sept. 1998 (special issue: "The Changing Educational Quality of the Workforce"), pp. 168–175.

Secretary's Commission on Achieving Necessary Skills. *What Work Requires of Schools: A SCANS Report for America 2000.* Washington, D.C.: U.S. Department of Labor, 1991.

Silvestri, G. T. "Occupational Employment Projections to 2006." *Monthly Labor Review,* 1997, *120*(11), 58–83.

Task Force on High-Performance Work and Workers: The Academic Connection. *Higher Education and Work Readiness: The View from the Corporation.* Washington, D.C.: Business–Higher Education Forum, Sept. 1995.

Task Force on High-Performance Work and Workers: The Academic Connection. *Spanning the Chasm: Corporate and Academic Cooperation to Improve Work-Force Preparation.* Washington, D.C.: Business–Higher Education Forum, Jan. 1997.

U.S. Department of Commerce, U.S. Department of Education, U.S. Department of Labor, National Institute of Literacy, and the Small Business Administration. *21st Century*

Skills for 21st Century Jobs. Washington, D.C.: U.S. Government Printing Office, Jan. 1999. [www.vpskillsummit.org].

Zemsky, R., and Cappelli, P. (eds.). "The Changing Educational Quality of the Workforce." *Annals of the American Academy of Political and Social Science,* Sept. 1998 (entire issue).

Zemsky, R., Shapiro, D., Iannozzi, M., Cappelli, P., and Bailey, T. *The Transition from Initial Education to Working Life in the United States of America: A Report to the Organisation for Economic Co-operation and Development (OECD) as Part of a Comparative Study of Transitions from Initial Education to Working Life in 14 Member Countries.* [http://www.irhe.upenn.edu/centers/oecd.html]. Oct. 1998.

KAREN PAULSON *is research associate at the National Center for Higher Education Management Systems in Boulder, Colorado.*

5

Testing is frequently used to determine competency levels. The rationale and the procedures for determining the standard, or passing level, on assessment instruments are the foci of this chapter. An example is presented, using the Bookmark procedure with a Web-based assessment measure of information-seeking skills.

Standard Setting

T. Dary Erwin, Steven L. Wise

How high is enough? What rating should a test taker obtain to be deemed adequate? What score is sufficient to certify that an individual knows the material or is able to perform the tasks being measured? What standards should educators espouse? Though the focus on collegiate assessment is usually about the definition or meaning of educational purposes and objectives or about the measurement of these objectives, another issue looms nearby, which is requiring full attention to standards. Who has not read about the need for standards from the public and employers? Standards are commonly mentioned among faculty; however, the current-day high-stakes consequences of assessment demand more exacting, technically sound, and credible implementation procedures.

As higher education assessment keeps moving from improvement to accountability, assessment practitioners, institutional researchers, and faculty should know how to set legally defensible standards using systematically followed procedures. This chapter describes the need for establishing these standards and outlines two methods that practitioners can use to set standards. Examples of standard setting are given in the information-seeking skills area of general education.

Standards in K–12

Faculty and institutional researchers are wise to follow the national political rhetoric in K–12 education as a harbinger of similar requirements in collegiate assessment. Most states have competency-testing policies in place for their elementary and secondary schools. Although testing critics cite a disparate impact against minorities, an overfocus on total scores versus more diagnostic subscores, and an artificial dichotomization of continuous variables (Jaeger, 1989), it is clear that competency testing has continued. In K–12 education, testing and standards are typically cast side by side. The state and national political scene continues to reverberate with loud rhetoric about standards and competency testing. It has become routine for candidates from both major political parties to advocate more accountability and higher standards in education. Business and industry particularly support greater accountability and clearer standards in higher education. For the public and government officials, competency testing serves or is perceived as serving various societal needs. Some of these needs include the following: *simpler reporting,* such as a pass or fail mark, to eliminate confusion about scores and their meaning; individual *development of knowledge and skills* to ensure the ability to function independently and successfully (Jaeger, 1989, p. 489); a *minimum standard of achievement* to guarantee this proper functioning; and the sense that there is a measure of *control and accountability.*

The use of standards in high school competency tests has been defended in the courts (Sireci and Green, 2000) as long as sound standard-setting procedures are followed. Cizek (1996) recommends documentation of a comprehensive standard-setting process to include the following: the selection process and expertise of subject matter review experts, the choice of a standard-setting method (two of which are illustrated later in this chapter), and independent evidence that the passing score or rating is reasonable.

Minimum Competency in Higher Education

Although higher education tends to concentrate on assessment for improvement of teaching and learning, assessment for accountability is potentially a stronger driving force for current and future practice. One finding from Steele and Lutz's state-by-state surveys (1995) notes that the legislature and public were calling for greater accountability, not necessarily improvement (Nettles, Cole, and Sharp, 1997, p. 19).

The application of standards to particular curricular areas is still somewhat limited. Policymakers have focused primarily on general education and basic skills assessment, not on assessment in the major or in student affairs. For examples of assessment efforts in general education, see the National Postsecondary Education Cooperative's review of collegiate-level critical-thinking, problem-solving, and writing-assessment instruments (nces.ed.gov/npec/evaltests).

Early assessment efforts in Florida and New Jersey utilized standards, or passing scores, in basic skills areas for individual student progression. In a process similar to that of professional licensure exams, entering New Jersey freshmen and Florida juniors have to meet designated cutoff score levels to advance educationally. Minimum standards of competency ensure that certain abilities are guaranteed, at least in the minds of the officials and the public who push for standards.

Although Nettles, Cole, and Sharp (1997) report that just 15 percent of the states mandate common, collegiate-level assessment instruments, ten other state boards now are considering their adoption. The Steele and Lutz (1995) survey of state higher education agencies also found that future policies were under way to mandate adequate skill and knowledge levels and clear demonstration of status of student learning. With the current climate toward clearer reporting of assessment results, therefore, it may be preemptive and certainly prudent for institutions to establish their own standards before forces outside of higher education impose them.

Higher education in the United States is not alone in its embracing of standards in the public policy area (Gaither, 1998). For instance, the Dearing Report outlines new directions for British higher education, "[Although] it would be impractical and undesirable to try to achieve close matching of standards across the whole of [British] higher education in all its diversity, it is nonetheless practicable to develop threshold or minimum standards, which set an agreed level of expectations of award, and we are convinced this should be done now" (Dearing, 1997, p. 156). Tapper and Salter (1998) report similar rhetoric in Japan and Australia, and uses of such terms as *standards, benchmarking*, and *thresholds* are frequently mentioned abroad (Erwin, 1999). The Western Governors University, which is supported by seventeen states or U.S. territories, uses a competency-based approach in combination with technologically delivered instruction. No grades are given, but students must pass assessment instruments at the end of the program for their degree. How students learn the instructional material does not matter in one sense; what matters primarily is the demonstration of the knowledge and skill domain of the respective academic program (Bankirer and Testa, 1999).

Standard setting is not limited to undergraduates. The proliferation of postbaccalaureate certificates and the certifying of competence in specialized and technical areas are escalating. The U.S. Department of Education currently tracks more than two thousand postbaccalaureate certificates, and the Council of Graduate Schools notes that several hundred are at the graduate level (Irby, 1999). To external and internal audiences, judgments about the quality of these certificates are tied directly to the credibility of the standard.

Besides using standards to certify individual students, higher education also uses standards to measure program or institutional performance by analyzing the percentage of students reaching the designated standard. Value-added analytical strategies may show great change in student learning over time, but minimum competency ensures that students have met statewide expectations through a passing score. Reporting the percentage of students reaching a given score or rating-scale level also implies a quick read on program effectiveness, program difficulty, or perhaps student preparation. Percentages, though occasionally misinterpreted, are a simple reporting statistic with which the public and lay constituents are comfortable. History shows that the rise of assessment was partially motivated by the lack of credibility

Angoff's Method Versus Bookmarking

The following sections will describe two standard-setting procedures currently in use. The first, called Angoff's method, is one of the oldest, most popular, and most extensively researched methods used. The second, the Bookmark procedure, is relatively new but holds substantial promise as an effective standard-setting method. More extensive discussions of standard-setting methods can be found in Cizek (1996) and Jaeger (1989).

Angoff's Method. In Angoff's method (1971), each judge is provided guidance on the conceptualization of a minimally competent examinee, asked to review the set of test or rating-scale items, and then estimate the probability that a minimally acceptable examinee would answer each item correctly. The sum of these probabilities across items would represent that judge's minimally acceptable score. In a highly simplified example, if there were a hundred items on the test, and a judge believed that a minimally acceptable examinee would have a 50 percent probability of passing each of the items, then the indicated minimally acceptable score for that judge would be $100 \times .50 = 50$. These probability values next would be averaged across judges to identify the consensus for a minimally acceptable score. The outcome of this procedure would be a subjective estimate of the expected test or scale performance of a minimally acceptable examinee.

In practice, Angoff's method has been modified in attempts to improve it. In one modification, judges are asked to make two or more rounds of ratings, with opportunities to discuss their probability judgments and then adjust those choices. An additional modification, when multiple rating rounds are used, is to provide judges with data that convey the impact—that is, the percentage of previous examinees who would have failed if a particular passing standard had been applied. The judges might then choose to adjust their probability ratings in response. Consequently, when one reads that a modified Angoff procedure was used to set a particular standard, one can infer that the authors might mean multiple judgment rounds, the provision of impact data, or both.

Despite its popularity and ease of implementation, Angoff's method has its critics. Its chief shortcoming is its dependence on judges making probability assignments on item performance. A number of studies (see, for example, Tversky and Kahneman, 1974) demonstrate the difficulty in accurately judging probabilities. Given that judges are being asked to estimate the probability of passing an item by a hypothetical examinee, a conceptualization based on the basis of a written definition of competence, one might well be skeptical of the resulting item ratings. Hence judges under Angoff's method are asked to render judgments for which they may be ill equipped. Assessment professionals and institutional researchers wishing to use this method should do so with caution. The previously mentioned criticism of Angoff's method reminds us that educators rarely, if ever, have an unambiguous criterion for evaluating the validity of a passing standard. Standard setting is a subjective process, and the best assessment practice is to try to ensure that the tasks given to judges are reasonable.

The Bookmark Procedure. A newer standard-setting method has emerged that deserves consideration by those assessment practitioners who need to set passing standards. In the Bookmark procedure (Lewis and others, 1998), judges are provided a set of test or rating-scale items that have been ordered in difficulty from easiest to hardest. This ordering is determined by ranking items from previous test administrations. The set of judges is divided into groups, typically three or four, and the judges themselves are asked to take the test prior to the standard-setting session.

There are three rating rounds to the Bookmark procedure. In the first round, the judges break into their groups and discuss the ordered items, one at a time. For each item, they answer the following questions: What does this item measure? And what makes this item harder than the items that precede it? After the groups have discussed the items, the judges individually make their first rating. Because the items have been ordered in difficulty (and hence require increasing proficiency for examinees to answer correctly), the judges are asked to identify the initial point in the item ordering that if an examinee knew the correct answer to all of the items that preceded that point, the examinee would have provided sufficient evidence that he or she had met the predefined threshold of competence.

In the second rating round, each judge is given the ratings of everyone in his or her group, and the groups discuss the differences among members' ratings. After this discussion, each judge provides a second rating of the amount of ordered item evidence needed to meet the definition of competence. In the third round, each judge is given the median rating given by each of the groups, the median rating of all of the judges, and impact data regarding how many examinees would have failed had the overall median been used to generate a passing score. The judges then discuss the differences among the medians of the groups and then, possibly taking into account the impact of the overall median, individually make their third ratings.

The overall median from the third round is used to generate the recommended passing score using item response theory (IRT). IRT is a modern measurement approach based on the probability of an examinee correctly responding to an item given the interaction between examinee ability and item characteristics such as item difficulty and discrimination. IRT scaling methods are beyond the scope of this chapter, but further information may be found in Hambleton, Swaminathan, and Rogers (1991). This cutoff recommendation is then forwarded to the person, committee, or board that is responsible for making the final passing-standard decision.

The Bookmark procedure has several advantages over Angoff's method. First, the task given to judges is more reasonable. Judges determine the amount of evidence needed to satisfy the definition of competence rather than estimating a set of probabilities. Second, the abstract notion of a hypothetical, minimally competent examinee is unnecessary. Third, the Bookmark procedure can be used with a wider variety of scoring options, including those that have more than two score points or dichotomous right or wrong scoring per tester scale item. Graded response, partial credit weighting, and polyotomous scoring options are currently popular. The Center for Assessment and Research Studies (CARS) at James Madison University (JMU) has adopted the Bookmark procedure as the standard-setting method of choice.

Example of the Bookmark Procedure. An example should help illustrate the use of the Bookmark procedure. At JMU, freshmen have to pass the Information-Seeking Skills Test (ISST), a computer-based information literacy test that is used as part of JMU's general education program. The ISST consists of fifty-three multiple-choice items. In the summer of 1999, a panel of twelve faculty judges was assembled to recommend a passing standard on the ISST to the JMU General Education Council. Before the one-day standard-setting session was convened, the judges took the ISST to familiarize themselves with the test items under realistic test-taking conditions. These faculty were then divided into three groups and were guided through the Bookmark procedure by two CARS assessment professionals at JMU.

Table 5.1 reveals that the judges' ratings converged across the three rounds. There was an eighteen-point range of ratings at round one, which decreased to a ten-point difference at round three. Clearly, judges were affected in different ways by the discussions in rounds two and three. From the first to the third rounds, four judges' ratings increased, three decreased, and five remained the same. The recommendation from the standard-setting procedure was a relatively high passing standard of forty-two on the fifty-three-item test, which was subsequently adopted by the General Education Council. The impact data indicated that had the indicated passing standard been used with the previous year's freshmen, only 57 percent would have passed the ISST on the first attempt. It was interesting to observe that the judges appeared comfortable with this low percentage, apparently concluding that improved instruction was needed rather than a lower passing standard. Indeed there appears to be improvement; during the 1999–2000 academic year, 84 percent of JMU freshmen had passed the ISST by May, with the remainder expected to do so by the end of the summer. At the end of the standard-setting session, the judges were asked to evaluate the process in which they had just participated. High satisfaction with the process and the passing-standard recommendation was expressed by the group. As the reader might note, a very positive feature of the Bookmark procedure is heavy faculty participation.

Summary

The rationale and two procedures, a traditional procedure and a new procedure, for standard setting are presented in this chapter. The Angoff and Bookmark procedures were outlined, with an example of judges' reactions through three rounds of discussions with the Bookmark procedure. The

**Table 5.1. Bookmark Procedure Ratings Given by Twelve
Judges to the Ordered ISST Items**

Judge	Group	Round One Rating	Round Two Rating	Round Three Rating
1	1	42	38	39
2	1	25	36	36
3	1	26	37	38
4	1	36	36	36
5	2	34	34	34
6	2	37	37	37
7	2	27	30	30
8	2	34	34	35
9	3	35	35	35
10	3	42	39	39
11	3	39	39	39
12	3	40	40	39

advantages of data-based minimum-competency determination, wide faculty participation, and ease of use were noted. Assessment professionals and institutional researchers will likely find the Bookmark procedure, in particular, of great benefit in their work.

As the stakes of assessment rise and as resources are increasingly linked to quality, the need grows for more formal and sophisticated assessment measures and analyses about quality. Assessment professionals and institutional researchers increasingly use a variety of quantitative and technical tools to apply in appropriate situations. Standard setting is one of those visible contexts requiring fair and systematic review mechanisms; assessment practitioners must be able to defend designated standards against expected challenges. Our ability to apply appropriate measurement and statistical techniques, as well as learning and developmental theories, is necessary not only at the institutional level but also for higher education as a whole. Our critics claim that our methods of determining quality are absent or faulty; consequently, higher education's credibility for determining and reporting accurate public information is under close scrutiny.

Part of the steady advancement associated with greater accountability points toward an increasing use of standards for public reporting. How higher education responds is crucial. Higher education has already been asked to state more clearly our educational objectives and to furnish assessment evidence of quality. How well each college and university does is now being translated into how many students reach a standard. If an institution outlines the source and meaning of its standards, then that institution is more likely to gain the public trust. To resist outside calls for standards is to invite noneducators to set standards for us, with results that will satisfy few of us. It is our duty as assessment professionals and institutional researchers to guide our fellow faculty, administrators, and staff in documenting and reporting credible assessment information about quality. At present, standards and standard setting are among the most visible fronts on which our work is needed and will be evaluated. It is an opportunity for us to seize.

References

Angoff, W. H. "Scales, Norms, and Equivalent Scores." In R. L. Thorndike (ed.), *Educational Measurement*. Washington, D.C.: American Council on Education, 1971.

Bankirer, M. W., and Testa, A. "Update on Assessment at Western Governors University." *Journal of Quality Management in Adult-Centered Management*, 1999, *9*(1), 13–14, 18.

Berk, R. A. "A Consumer's Guide to Setting Performance Standards on Criterion-Referenced Tests." *Review of Educational Research*, 1986, *56*, 137–172.

Cizek, G. J. "Standard Setting Guidelines." *Educational Measurement: Issues and Practice*, 1996, *15*(2), 20–31.

Dearing, R. *Higher Education in the Learning Society: Report of the National Committee*. London: Her Majesty's Stationery Office, 1997. [www.ex.ac.uk/dearing.html].

Erwin, T. D. "United States Perspective and Experiences on Performance Indicators and Threshold Standards: How Is Quality Determined?" In H. Smith, M. Armstrong, and S. Brown (eds.), *Benchmarks and Threshold Standards in Higher Education*. London: Kogan Page, 1999.

Gaither, G. H. *Quality Assurance in Higher Education: An International Perspective*. San Francisco: Jossey-Bass, 1998.

Hambleton, R. K., Swaminathan, H., and Rogers, H. J. *Fundamentals of Item Response Theory*. Thousand Oaks, Calif.: Sage, 1991.

Irby, A. J. "Postbaccalaureate Certificates: Higher Education's Growth Market." *Change*, Mar.–Apr. 1999, *31*(2), 36–41.

Jaeger, R. M. "Certifying Student Competence." In R. L. Linn (ed.), *Educational Measurement*. (3rd ed.) New York: American Council on Education, 1989.

Lewis, D. M., and others. "The Bookmark Standard Setting Procedure: Methodology and Recent Implementations." Paper presented at the annual meeting of the National Council on Measurement in Education, San Diego, Calif., Apr. 1998.

Nettles, M., Cole, J.J.K., and Sharp, S. *Benchmarking Assessment: State Governing, Coordinating Board, and Regional Accreditation Association Policies and Practices*. Ann Arbor, Mich.: Center for the Study of Higher and Postsecondary Education, 1997.

Sireci, S. G., and Green, P. C. "Legal and Psychometric Criteria for Evaluating Teacher Certification Tests." *Educational Measurement: Issues and Practice*, 2000, *19*(1), 22–34.

Steele, J. M., and Lutz, D. A. *Report of American College Testing's (ACT) Research on Postsecondary Assessment Needs*. Iowa City, Iowa: American College Testing, 1995.

Tapper, E. R., and Salter, B. G. "The Dearing Report and the Maintenance of Academic Standards: Towards a New Academic Corporatism." *Higher Education Quarterly*, 1998, *52*(1), 22–34.

Tversky, A., and Kahneman, D. "Judgment Under Uncertainty: Heuristics and Biases." *Science*, 1974, *185*, 1124–1131.

T. DARY ERWIN is director of the Center for Assessment and Research Studies and professor of psychology at James Madison University, Harrisonburg, Virginia.

STEVEN L. WISE is senior assessment specialist and professor of psychology at James Madison University, Harrisonburg, Virginia.

6

Accreditors of all stripes carry at least some expectations that institutions seeking affiliation status will be able to explain and document their outcomes in ways that address student learning. Nowhere is that focus more often applied than in the emerging area of distance education.

Competencies, Regional Accreditation, and Distance Education: An Evolving Role?

Dawn Geronimo Terkla

Accrediting associations and the institutions they oversee have shared interests in accountability. The metric for accountability gradually has begun the shift from institutional inputs toward institutional outputs, a process that dates to at least two decades ago, when the Carnegie Foundation for the Advancement of Teaching (1982) urged that learning outcomes be incorporated in accreditation processes. Full implementation, however, has been decidedly slow in arriving. Despite recent progress in documenting student learning, the competency-based movement has been more firmly embraced by entities outside of the traditional higher education mainstream. Even so, accreditors of all stripes carry at least some expectations that institutions seeking affiliation status will be able to explain and document their outcomes in ways that address student learning. Nowhere is that focus more applied than in the emerging area of distance education.

This chapter provides the reader with an overview of how competencies are linked to current accreditation standards and suggests techniques that institutional researchers can employ to position their institutions in the accreditation process. Particular focus is given in this chapter to the standards that make reference to competencies among the six regional accrediting associations. Current accreditation standards addressing competencies among regional accreditors are not yet uniform, and the degree of their application to institutions varies from association to association. There are, however, commonalities among associations and some promising interregional efforts to develop consistent standards for accrediting distance education programs. Although specialized or professional accreditation entities

New Directions for Institutional Research, no. 110, Summer 2001   © John Wiley & Sons, Inc.

make more direct use of specific learning competencies because the focus is more narrow, regional accreditors exercise the most sway over the *total* institution. Readers wishing a more developed treatment of the role of professional or industry-specific accreditation should consult the chapters in this volume by Paulson and Bedard Voorhees.

The public has demonstrated an appetite for institutional accountability. Matthews (1998) argues that a learning outcome, as measured by student competency, is the quality measure that makes the most sense to consumers. This rising tide of questioning spills over directly into fundamental questions of institutional credibility and whether institutions can effectively and appropriately respond with the data and information. This issue was at the forefront of the discussion among educators during the creation of a new model of accreditation promulgated by the Western Association of Schools and Colleges Accrediting Commission for Senior Colleges and Universities: "Accreditation stands as a distinctive American innovation to assure quality in higher education. It was founded more than 100 years ago on the principle of peer review, meaning that those within the academy are best able to evaluate the quality of higher education institutions. In the past decades, however, both institutions and the challenges of defining and quality have become significantly more complex and come under increasing scrutiny" (Western Association of Schools and Colleges Accrediting Commission for Senior Colleges and Universities, *Handbook of Accreditation 2000,* p. 2).

External scrutiny of regional accreditors constitutes a true watershed for higher education. This scrutiny perhaps has been brought about by the popularization of distance education and the access to higher education opportunity that it promises. Never before have institutions and accrediting associations been forced to examine the connections between the way in which they produce learning and the demands of educational consumers. In the electronic age, the public grows more restive with prolonged educational experiences that are planned more for the convenience of institutions than for the convenience of individual learners. The nexus among competencies, distance education, and accreditation is newly plowed ground, but an acreage that is expanding exponentially as most institutions are faced with the need to change in order to capture new markets.

Few institutions at the turn of this century can claim to be totally competency based. Notable exceptions are Western Governors University and Alverno College. Many other institutions, however, lay claim to outcome-based approaches for at least some components of institutional activity, especially during accreditation review. The emerging activity in programs designed specifically for adult degree completion, many of which are conducted at a distance, and increasing institutional activity in distance education itself bring new focus to competencies, especially because in a virtual campus environment there may be little else for accreditors to review. Moving away from credit hours and seat time toward the demonstration of competencies requires techniques and changes in institutional culture that are addressed elsewhere in this volume. With this backdrop, institutional researchers must be prepared to respond on behalf of at least some or perhaps all parts of the institution to questions of quality that are the pivot point for accreditation review. In most cases, they must lead institutional efforts to demonstrate, either quantitatively or qualitatively, that the goals and objectives espoused by the institution are being achieved. In the realm of student learning, such responsibilities are not easily met.

The Meaning of Accreditation

There are two basic types of educational accreditation, *institutional* and *specialized*, or *programmatic*. Institutional accreditation normally applies to an entire institution, indicating that each of an institution's components is contributing to the achievement of the institution's objectives, although not necessarily all at the same level of quality. The various commissions of the regional accrediting associations, for example, perform institutional accreditation, as do many national accrediting agencies. Specialized or programmatic accreditation normally applies to programs, departments, or schools that are parts of an institution. The accredited unit may be as large as a college or school within a university or as small as a curriculum within a discipline. Most of the specialized or programmatic accrediting agencies review units within an institution of higher education that are accredited by one of the regional accrediting commissions. Certain accrediting agencies also accredit professional schools, such as medical, dental, and law schools, and other specialized or vocational institutions of higher education, meaning that a specialized or programmatic accrediting agency may also function in the capacity of an institutional accrediting agency. In addition, a number of specialized accrediting agencies accredit educational programs in noneducational settings such as hospitals.[1]

The U.S. Secretary of Education is required by statute to publish a list of nationally recognized accrediting agencies that the secretary determines to be reliable authorities on the quality of education or training provided by the institutions of higher education and the higher education programs they accredit. Most institutions attain eligibility for federal funds by holding accredited or preaccredited status with one of the accrediting agencies recognized by the secretary, in addition to fulfilling other eligibility requirements. For example, accreditation by a nationally recognized institutional accrediting agency enables the institutions it accredits to establish eligibility to participate in the federal student financial assistance programs administered by the U.S. Department of Education under Title IV of the Higher Education Act of 1965 as amended.

Currently, six regional accrediting bodies maintain eight separate commissions that deal directly with accrediting postsecondary institutions:

Middle States Association of Colleges and Schools (Commission on Higher Education), New England Association of Schools and Colleges (Commission on Institutions of Higher Education and Commission on Technical and Career Institutions), North Central Association of Schools and Colleges (Commission on Institutions of Higher Education), Northwest Association of Schools and Colleges (Commission on Colleges), Southern Association of Colleges and Schools (Commission on Colleges), and Western Association of Schools and Colleges (Accrediting Commission for Community and Junior Colleges and Accrediting Commission for Senior Colleges and Universities). For purposes of financial aid eligibility, the U.S. Secretary of Education also recognizes more than fifty other institutional and specialized accrediting bodies, ranging in purview from acupuncture and oriental medicine to veterinary medicine, and including, for example, Bible college education, funeral service education, radiological technology, and teacher education. These professional accrediting agencies play a major role in shaping the content and operation of individual programs in institutions (for example, the American Association of Colleges and Schools of Business, the American Bar Association, the American Council on Pharmaceutical Education, the American Library Association, the American Psychological Association, the Commission on Collegiate Nursing Education, and the National Council for Accreditation of Teacher Education). Successful affiliation with these professional associations may or may not result in a specific program's eligibility to participate in Title IV programs.

Regional Accrediting Associations and Competency Expectations

Although regional accreditors have no legal control over educational institutions, they promulgate standards of quality or criteria of institutional excellence and approve or admit to membership those institutions that meet the standards or criteria. Although all regional accrediting bodies promulgate standards that embrace student learning, such language is not consistent, nor does it uniformly use competencies as a reference point. The intensity of the language and the level of prescription vary from region to region.

Middle States Association of Colleges and Schools Commission on Higher Education. The *Characteristics of Excellence in Higher Education: Standards for Accreditation* was approved by Middle States in 1993 (Middle States Association of Colleges and Schools Commission on Higher Education, 1994). The Middle States standards are the least explicit among the regional accreditors and do not focus specifically on competencies. At the macro level of meaning, however, the language in the standards makes it clear that institutions have to identify institution-specific goals and to demonstrate that they are being achieved. References to student learning are found in the language cited in the following excerpts.

These common characteristics of excellence are the standards by which the Commission on Higher Education determines an institution's accreditation: programs and courses which develop general intellectual skills such as the ability to form independent judgement, to weigh values, to understand fundamental theory, and to interact effectively in a culturally diverse world. [p. 4]

Institutions should develop guidelines and procedures for assessing their overall effectiveness as well as student learning outcomes. [p. 6]

Mission, Goals and Objectives: Educational goals need to be stated in terms of outcomes they seek to achieve, e.g., the changes and/or competencies they seek to foster in their students. [p. 7]

The Middle States standards now are under revision, and new standards for accrediting colleges and universities will go into effect in February 2002. At this time, the commission has invited comments on the proposed revisions. According to the Fall 2000 Middle States Commission newsletter, the new standards place a greater emphasis on student learning in an effort to improve quality assurance, focusing more on results than on inputs and processes (http://www.msache.org/pubs.html). The new standards will first be applied to those institutions that are scheduled for review in the 2003–04 academic year.

New England Association of Schools and Colleges (NEASC) Commission on Institutions of Higher Education. Adopted most recently in 1992, Standard Four, Programs and Instructions, deals most directly with issues of competency (New England Association of Schools and Colleges Commission on Institutions of Higher Education, 1998). These standards clearly state specific areas in which students should be competent.

Standard 4.18. The major or area of concentration affords the student the opportunity to develop knowledge and skills in a specific disciplinary or interdisciplinary area above the introductory level, through properly sequenced course work. Requirements for the major area of concentration are based on clearly defined and articulated learning objectives, including mastery of the knowledge, methods, and theories pertinent to a particular area of inquiry. [p. 8]

Standard 4.19. Graduates successfully completing an undergraduate program demonstrate competence in written and oral communication in English; the ability for scientific and quantitative reasoning, for critical analysis and logical thinking; and the capability for continuing learning. They also demonstrate knowledge and understanding of scientific, historical, and social phenomena, and a knowledge and appreciation of aesthetic and ethical dimensions of humankind. In addition, graduates demonstrate an in-depth understanding of an area of knowledge or practice and its interrelatedness with other areas. [p. 9]

NEASC recently proposed revisions to the current standards. There are, however, no proposed changes to standards 4.18 and 4.19. Instead the proposed changes are primarily related to four areas: faculty, library, technology and distance education, and student services.

New England Association of Schools and Colleges Commission on Technical and Career Institutions. NEASC's Commission on Technical and Career Institutions does not use the term *competencies* in its *Standards of Membership for Institutions at the Technical or Career Level,* as revised in 1996 (New England Association of Schools and Colleges Commission on Technical and Career Institutions, 1996). Rather, the language is vague, leaving it to institutional discretion to identify appropriate learning objectives and demonstrate that the institutional-specific objectives are achieved.

> *Standard 2. Planning and Assessment.* The institution identifies and publishes in appropriate and accessible documents the expected learning outcomes for each of its major programs and general education programs. It assesses and documents that students completing its programs have achieved those stated learning outcomes. [p. 2]

> *Standard 7. Programs of Study.* The major program, through the development of a mastery of methods of inquiry, promotes an appreciation for the complex structure of the discipline, its relatedness to other knowledge, and current field practice. There is continuous progression across the discipline as well as depth beyond the introductory level. The timing, sequencing and delivery format of courses in a program ensure opportunities for reflection, analysis, mastery of the subject matter and the development of skills of application. [p. 8]

North Central Association (NCA) of Schools and Colleges Commission on Institutions of Higher Education. The North Central Association of Schools and Colleges Commission on Institutions of Higher Education publishes five criteria for accreditation (North Central Association of Schools and Colleges Commission on Institutions of Higher Education, 1999). These criteria were adopted in 1999. Criterion three has language that is directly related to student learning and assessment. There is a clear expectation on the part of the commission that institutions will demonstrate that students have achieved specific competencies and skills.

> *Criterion 3.* The institution is accomplishing its educational and other purposes. In determining appropriate patterns of evidence for this criterion, the Commission considers evidence such as . . . assessment of appropriate student academic achievement in all its programs, documenting . . . proficiency in skills and competencies essential for all college-educated adults; [and] mastery of the level of knowledge appropriate to the degree granted. [p. 3]

Northwest Association of Schools and Colleges Commission on Colleges. The current standards for the Northwest Association of Schools and Colleges Commission on Colleges were adopted in 1988 (Northwest Association of Schools and Colleges Commission on Colleges, 1999). Standard Two, Educational Program and Its Effectiveness, addresses specifically the requirement that students need to master competencies for independent learning.

> Baccalaureate and academic or transfer associate degree programs include a substantial core of general education instruction with identifiable outcomes and require competence in (a) written and oral communication, (b) quantitative reasoning, (c) critical analysis and logical thinking, and (d) literacy in the discourse or technology appropriate to the program of study. [pp. 2–3]

In 1992, the Northwest Association adopted language that included a list of outcomes measures, designed to be illustrative rather than prescriptive, that could be used in an effective outcomes assessment. The list included the following items: student information, midprogram assessments, end-of-program assessments, program review and specialized accreditation, alumni satisfaction and loyalty, dropouts and noncompleters, and employment and employer satisfaction measures (pp. 10–11). This list provides some evidence to show that this accrediting agency is moving toward the position that it is important to incorporate outcome measures in the accreditation process.

Southern Association of Colleges and Schools (SACS) Commission on Colleges. The SACS Commission on Colleges *Criteria for Accreditation* were approved in 1984 and modified in 1997 (Southern Association of Colleges and Schools Commission on Colleges, 1997). Section IV, Educational Programs, is most directly related to competencies. The language in this standard might lend itself to a competency-based evaluative approach.

> *Section IV.* [An institution] . . . prepares its students to function in an increasingly diverse, complex, and global society by imparting to them not only a mastery of a body of knowledge and technical skills but also by providing opportunities for them to develop enhanced communication skills and the ability to reason critically. [p. 23]

> 4.2.2. The institution must demonstrate that its graduates of degree programs are competent in reading, writing, oral communication, fundamental mathematical skills and basic use of computers. [p. 27]

Western Association of Schools and Colleges (WASC) Accrediting Commission for Community and Junior Colleges. WASC's Commission for Community and Junior Colleges is currently operating under standards of accreditation that were adopted in 1996 (Western Association of Schools and Colleges Accrediting Commission for Community and Junior Colleges, 2000). Standard Four, Educational Programs, deals directly with the area of student learning and competencies. In fact, there is substantial language in these standards that directly focuses on competency-based measures.

B. Degree and Certificate Programs

B.2. The institution identifies its degrees and certificates in ways which are consistent with the program content, degree objectives, and student mastery of knowledge and skills including, where appropriate, career preparation and competencies. [p. 4]

B.3. The institution identifies and makes public expected learning outcomes for its degree and certificate programs. Students completing programs demonstrate achievement of those stated learning outcomes. [p. 4]

B.5. Students completing degree programs demonstrate competence in the use of language and computation. [p. 4]

B.6. The institution documents the technical and professional competence of students completing its vocational and occupational programs. [p. 4]

C. General Education

C.4. Students completing the institution's general program demonstrate competence in oral and written communication, scientific and quantitative reasoning, and critical analysis/logical thinking. [p. 5]

Western Association of Schools and Colleges Accrediting Commission for Senior Colleges and Universities. In 1998, the WASC Commission for Senior Colleges and Universities began to redesign the accreditation process. At this writing, a draft of the *Handbook of Accreditation 2000* was available for review (Western Association of Schools and Colleges Accrediting Commission for Senior Colleges and Universities, 2000). Many of the revisions to this accreditation process were designed to make the exercise more proactive and to be more responsive to the public's desire for accountability. One of the espoused outcomes of the WASC accreditation is to promote deep institutional engagement with the issue of educational effectiveness and student learning and to develop and share good practices in assessing and improving the teaching and learning process (p. 8). The new WASC accreditation process includes four standards of accreditation that are framed by two core commitments—institutional capacity and educational effectiveness (p. 14). In this framework, WASC appears to move beyond courses and programs as the unit of analysis for generating competencies. Standard Two, Achieving Educational Objectives Through Core Functions, is most germane to this discussion.

2.2. All degrees, undergraduate and graduate, awarded by the institution are clearly defined in terms of entry-level requirements and in terms of levels of student achievement necessary for graduation that represent more than simply the accumulation of courses or credits.

Baccalaureate programs engage students in an integrated course of study of sufficient breadth and depth to prepare them for work, citizenship, and a fulfilling life. These programs also ensure the development of core learning abilities and competencies including, but not limited to, college-level written and oral communication, college-level quantitative skills, information literacy, and the habit of critical analysis of data and argument. In addition, baccalaureate programs actively foster an appreciation of diversity, civic responsibility, the ability to work with others, and the capability to engage in lifelong learning. Baccalaureate programs also ensure breadth for all students in the areas of cultural and aesthetic, social and political, as well as scientific and technical knowledge expected of educated persons in this society. Finally, students are required to engage in an in-depth, focused and sustained program of study as part of their baccalaureate programs. [p. 19]

2.7. In order to improve program currency and effectiveness, all programs offered by the institution are subject to review, including analyses of the achievement of the program's learning objectives and outcomes. Where appropriate, evidence from external constituencies such as employers and professional societies is included in such reviews. [p. 20]

These competency-based review standards are summarized in Table 6.1. It is clear that regional accrediting agencies are moving in the direction of requiring institutions to document that students have developed an expected set of core learning abilities and competencies before they graduate. It is probable that these statements may become uniform in the near term, especially as interregional standards for distance education are refined during the next several years.

Fundamentals of Competency-Based Accreditation Review

Most institutional accreditation reviews are intended to be comprehensive— that is, they seek to address the traditional elements of institutional functioning, including mission, program content, organizational structure, finances, human resources, and facilities. For most visiting regional accrediting teams, these elements constitute a wide swath of measurement points. Competency-based accreditation review, in contrast, would focus on the learning process and the outcomes of that process. This is not to suggest that the other, traditional elements of accreditation should be ignored.

Table 6.1. Summary of Competency-Based Requirements of Regional Accrediting Entities

Regional Accrediting Entity	Standard
Middle States Association of Colleges and Schools Commission on Higher Education	*Characteristic 6.* Programs and courses that develop general intellectual skills, such as the ability to form independent judgment, weigh values, understand fundamental theory, and interact in a culturally diverse world.
New England Association of Schools and Colleges Commission on Institutions of Higher Education	*Standard 4.18.* Mastery of the knowledge, methods, and theories pertinent to a particular area of inquiry. *Standard 4.19.* Demonstration of (a) competence in written and oral communication, (b) ability for scientific and quantitative reasoning, (c) ability for critical analysis and logical thinking, and (d) capability for continuing learning. Also demonstration of knowledge of scientific, historical, and social phenomena.
New England Association of Schools and Colleges Commission on Technical and Career Institutions	*Standard 2. Planning and Assessment.* The institution assesses and documents that students completing its programs have achieved its stated learning outcomes. *Standard 7. Programs of Study.* The major program, through the development of a mastery of methods of inquiry, promotes an appreciation for the complex structure of the discipline, its relatedness to other knowledge, and current field practice.
North Central Association of Schools and Colleges Commission on Institutions of Higher Education	*Criterion 3.* The institution is accomplishing its educational purposes as evidenced by documenting proficiency in skills and competencies and mastery of the appropriate level of knowledge.
Northwest Association of Schools and Colleges Commission on Colleges	*Standard 2.* Programs include a substantial core with identifiable outcomes and require competencies in (a) written and oral communication, (b) quantitative reasoning, (c) critical analysis and logical thinking, and (d) literacy in the discourse or technology appropriate to the program of study.

Southern Association of Colleges and Schools Commission on Colleges	*Section 4.2.2.* The institution must demonstrate that its graduates of degree programs are competent in reading, writing, oral communication, fundamental mathematical skills, and basic use of computers.
Western Association of Schools and Colleges Accrediting Commission for Community and Junior Colleges	*Standard B.2.* Mastery of knowledge and skills, including career preparation and competencies. *Standard B.3.* Completion of programs that demonstrate achievement of institution's stated learning outcomes. *Standard B.5.* Demonstration of competence in the use of language and computation. *Standard C.4.* Demonstration of competence in oral and written communication, scientific and quantitative reasoning, and critical analysis and logical thinking.
Western Association of Schools and Colleges Accrediting Commission for Senior Colleges and Universities	*Standard 2.2.* All programs ensure development of core learning abilities and competencies, including written and oral communication, quantitative skills, information literacy, critical analysis of data and argument; and foster appreciation of diversity, civic responsibility, ability to work with others, and the capability to engage in lifelong learning. *Standard 2.7.* All programs are subject to review, including analysis of the achievement of the program's learning objectives and outcomes.

Sources: Middle States Association of Colleges and Schools Commission on Higher Education, 1994; New England Association of Schools and Colleges Commission on Institutions of Higher Education, 1998; New England Association of Schools and Colleges Commission on Technical and Career Institutions, 1996; North Central Association of Schools and Colleges Commission on Institutions of Higher Education, 1999; Northwest Association of Schools and Colleges Commission on Colleges, 1999; Southern Association of Colleges and Schools Commission on Colleges, 1997; Western Association of Schools and Colleges Accrediting Commission for Community and Junior Colleges, 2000; Western Association of Schools and Colleges Accrediting Commission for Senior Colleges and Universities, 2000.

Rather, a competency-based review would apply sharp focus to the types of competencies that a given institution or entity seeks to produce.

For one reason or another, a significant number of institutions and learning organizations choose to forgo accreditation by one of the six regional bodies. This is particularly striking in the information technology field, where Adelman (2000) estimates a worldwide enrollment of 1.6 million students in programs leading to industry certification, a process that is almost exclusively performance based. Learners who can demonstrate proficiency through standardized examinations gain entry and advancement in this field regardless of the accredited status of the organization or entity that facilitated their learning. Although some higher education institutions have been active participants in this performance-based movement through collaborative arrangements with certifying organizations and employers, the burgeoning job market in information technology is wholly unaffected by regional accreditation—that is, the demands of the industry for specific competency certification have displaced the ability or inclination of regional accreditors to respond. The marketplace, instead, drives quality standards and determines who will be certified and under what conditions.

All learning providers, regardless of accreditation status, have learned to articulate their intention to produce certain types of student-related outcomes. The reluctance of those institutions operating outside the regional accrediting associations to participate in accreditation review might be overcome if the basis for the review itself were focused on competencies. At a minimum, uniform processes for reviewing competencies would level the playing field among all types of learning providers and supply the public with a valid yardstick to make comparisons among providers. In response to the new types of institutions entering the educational marketplace and to the increased demand for certifying quality among those providers of distance education whose operations transcend fixed boundaries, regional accrediting bodies have formed the Council for Regional Accrediting Commissions (CRAC). This council seeks to promote interregional dialogue and convergence on uniform processes for documenting quality.

Setting Universal Competency-Based Standards. By whatever form, the next generation of regional or interregional accreditation is likely to focus more specifically on student learning outcomes. Carnevale (2000) reports substantial progress among the regional accrediting bodies toward common agreement on guidelines for evaluating distance education. The Western Cooperative for Educational Telecommunications, a subunit of the Western Interstate Commission for Higher Education (WICHE), in cooperation with the eight regional accrediting commissions, developed draft guidelines, which are under review at this writing. They seek to set standards for granting accreditation to distance education programs and institutions (see http://www.wiche.edu/telecom/resources /publications/Guidelines.pdf for complete guidelines). These guidelines are commonly referred to as the WICHE Principles. These principles provide that no regional bodies would accredit a distance education program unless faculty members controlled the creation of the content, the institution provided technical and program support for both faculty members and students, and the program had evaluation and assessment methods for measuring student learning.

CRAC's Criteria for the Evaluation of Distance Education. The evaluation and assessment of distance education as proposed by CRAC's guidelines should be of considerable interest to institutional researchers who might seek to position their institution's participation in this arena. For example, these guidelines create the institutional obligation to engage in sustained, evidence-based, and participatory inquiry as to whether distance education programs are meeting their objectives. There is a clear focus on the student in these guidelines; although not all criteria apply to student learning and competencies, it is notable that the first criterion requires institutions to specify learning outcomes. CRAC has recommended that overall program effectiveness be determined by the following criteria. The enumeration of each criterion is followed by suggestions for institutional research personnel to provide leadership to address that criterion.

1. The extent to which student learning matches intended outcomes, including for degree programs, as both the goals of general education and the objectives of the major. This criterion calls for the explicit enumeration of intended learning outcomes and a match with assessment techniques to determine success. Institutional researchers should refer to the chapters by Bers and Bedard Voorhees in this volume for guidance on how to write competency statements in unambiguous ways, which can lead directly to their measurement.

2. The extent to which student intent is met. Institutional researchers need to be in the forefront in assisting programs to determine the intent of incoming students and to evaluate whether these initial goals are met. This is an often-overlooked area in outcome assessment. Accurate initial assessment leads to more informed measurement of subsequent enrollment patterns.[2]

3. Student retention rates, including variations over time. It is here that institutional researchers can aid their institution's distance education efforts by applying the profession's understanding of student retention and appropriate methodologies to measure retention. The key here is the incorporation of student intentions within the measurement scheme.

4. Student satisfaction, as measured by regular surveys. Institutional researchers have many resources from which to choose to address this criterion, including standardized questionnaires and homegrown surveys. A premium should be placed on administering these assessments on-line.

5. Faculty satisfaction, as measured by regular surveys and by formal and informal peer review processes. Not only will institutional researchers find the experiences of faculty who teach in distance education programs helpful in establishing program direction and refinement, but sharing the results of these surveys can assist other faculty to avoid the pitfalls inherent in distance offering.

6. The extent to which access is provided to students not previously served. Institutional researchers will need to familiarize themselves with market research and segmentation techniques to determine whether institutional efforts in distance education are providing access to the institution's program for those not otherwise likely to enroll. Here, it is critical to assess the financial structure of the distance education program and its relationship to the financial resources of enrollees to determine the existence of a digital divide.

7. Measures of the extent to which library and learning resources are used appropriately by the program's students. Institutional researchers should be involved in student's formative evaluation of distance education as well as summative efforts. Fulfillment of this criterion means a close collaboration between faculty expectations for use of the library or learning resources and institutional research's ability to verify that use.

8. Measures of student competence in fundamental skills, such as communication, comprehension, and analysis. It is here that the lessons provided by this volume can be directly applied. Institutional researchers will need to work directly with faculty to isolate these competencies in ways that lead most efficiently to their measurement. Key here is the extent to which the institution's traditional practices for assessing these skills have been deployed in its distance education efforts. Although both on-campus and virtual programs can be conceptually in synchronization, the lack of proximity of students to the traditional campus can pose special burdens on efforts to assess levels of competency, especially when direct supervision of the assessment activity is desired.

9. Cost-effectiveness of the program to its students, as compared with campus-based activities. Technology is a tool that can really enable people to learn in their own way, but there is an inevitable price tag. Institutional researchers can assist other campus decision makers with techniques to analyze the cost-effectiveness of distance education. For example, the frequently held perception is that the initial costs of program development require significant onetime expenditures but that these developmental costs gradually recede after implementation. Legislators also are interested in the perception that the overall lower costs of distance education will result in significant decreases in appropriations. Finally, what are the limits of what students in the distance education market will bear by way of tuition and fees if the convenience of learning anytime, anywhere, anyplace, and anyhow is a paramount concern in their lives?

Other Tools for Competency-Based Accreditation. The criteria proposed by CRAC are consistent with the lessons learned in a recent pilot study on competency-based accreditation. Conducted by the National Center for Higher Education Management Systems (2000) on behalf of the Council for Higher Education Accreditation (CHEA), this study points to the pitfalls and opportunities inherent in transforming traditional accreditation processes. This report is an outgrowth of a pilot project examining Western Governors University and the need to apply accreditation tools in ways that examine the quality of an outcome-based institution that is also electronically based. The pilot study used the traditional framework for a site-based accreditation review—namely, a self-study, peer review, and a site visit, followed by a team report with recommendations. However, the processes for assessing the quality of a competency-based model require much different tools.

The tools that the CHEA report found fundamental for performing a competency-based review are enumerated in the following discussion. Consistent with the CRAC recommendations, student learning in the form of competency-based curriculum is paramount. Following each tool are advice and recommendations to institutional researchers about how to facilitate such reviews.

1. Standards that call for documentation of student competencies and documentation of organizational capacity to sustain competency-based curriculum and services. Although this is a consistent theme throughout the present volume, institutional researchers should particularly consult the chapter by Bers on measuring and reporting competencies for practical advice on documentation. Organizational capacity is a direct product of faculty buy-in and the feedback loops to curricular improvement. See Jones's chapter in this volume on transforming curricula for specific techniques to promote sustainability of institutional change.

2. Scoring instruments, or guides, to be used by the review team to make judgments about institutional performance. Interestingly, these guides, or rubrics, can be developed consistently across programs using techniques similar to those depicted by Erwin and Wise in their chapter in this volume on standard setting. The competency-based review team in this instance is analogous to faculty groups who must determine what is a competency and how it might unambiguously be measured. Development of clear standards in this area prior to a review team's arrival is fertile ground for institutional researchers and can aid the institution in reaching internal consensus about institutional performance.

3. An institutional portfolio of existing institutional data to provide evidence that the competency-based standards have been met. When key decisions have been made about the standards that are to be evaluated, institutional researchers will likely be charged with preparing these data. Ideally, this process will begin during the time that internal standards are first developed and not later as the prospect of the review team's arrival looms. These data should be collected routinely. The data sources mentioned in the CRAC criteria discussed previously are an excellent place to start, especially the amassing of information about student competency attainment.

Summary

The lessons that have been learned from the movement toward institutional outcomes have influenced the delivery of competency-based models. Certainly, the stage is well prepared for further implementation of competency-based accreditation. The emergence and acceptance of competency-based accreditation review appear well under way in the field of distance education. The extent to which distance education can truly transform the educational process will determine in large part the future commitment of regional accreditors to full-scale competency review. In the meantime, institutional researchers might do well to examine both their regional accrediting body's expectations for measuring student learning and those of any specialized accrediting bodies to which their institution subscribes. The techniques described in this chapter and elsewhere in this volume can arm institutional researchers with valuable resources that may be applied to standard accreditation as well as reviews of distance education. Application of at least some of the competency-based accreditation techniques identified in this volume is a viable solution to documenting outcomes and demonstrating the quality of a student's educational experience. Through a diligent process connected to the accreditation process, it may be quite possible that institutions can turn the tide regarding credibility by responding effectively to questions of student competence with focused information.

Notes

1. A comprehensive listing of professional and specialized accreditation may be found in *Quality Review: Council for Higher Education Accreditation Almanac of External Quality Review* (Council for Higher Education Accreditation, 1999).
2. See Voorhees and Zhou (2000) for a fuller treatment of how student intentions influence subsequent measurement of student success, especially among community college students.

References

Adelman, C. *A Parallel Postsecondary Universe: The Certification System in Information Technology.* Washington, D.C.: U.S. Department of Education, Office of Educational Research and Improvement, 2000.
Carnegie Foundation for the Advancement of Teaching. *The Control of the Campus.* Princeton, N.J.: Princeton University Press, 1982.
Carnevale, D. "Accrediting Bodies Consider New Standards for Distance Education Programs." *Chronicle of Higher Education,* 2000, 47(2), A58–A59.
Council for Higher Education Accreditation. *Quality Review: Council for Higher Education Accreditation Almanac of External Quality Review.* Washington, D.C.: Council for Higher Education Accreditation, 1999.
Matthews, D. "Transforming Higher Education: Implications for State Higher Education Finance Policy." *Educom Review,* 1998, 33(5), 48–57.
Middle States Association of Colleges and Schools Commission on Higher Education. *Characteristics of Excellence in Higher Education: Standards for Accreditation.* [http://www.msache.org/msachar.pdf]. Feb. 1994.
National Center for Higher Education Management Systems. *The Competency Standards Project: Another Approach to Accreditation Review.* Washington, D.C.: Council for Higher Education Accreditation, 2000.
New England Association of Schools and Colleges Commission on Institutions of Higher Education. *Standards for Accreditation.* [http://www.neasc.org/cihe/stancihe.htm]. 1998.

New England Association of Schools and Colleges Commission on Technical and Career Institutions. *Standards of Membership for Institutions at the Technical or Career Level.* [http://www.neasc.org/ctci/stantche.htm]. 1996.
North Central Association of Schools and Colleges Commission on Institutions of Higher Education. *The Criteria for Accreditation.* [http://www.ncahigherlearningcommission.org/overview/ovcriteria.html]. 1999.
Northwest Association of Schools and Colleges Commission on Colleges. *Standards.* [http://www.cocnasc.org.policyprocedure.standards.htm]. 1999.
Southern Association of Colleges and Schools Commission on Colleges. *Criteria for Accreditation.* [http://www.sacscoc.org/COC/criteria.htm]. 1997.
Voorhees, R. A., and Zhou, D. "Intentions and Goals at the Community College: Associating Student Perceptions and Demographics." *Community College Journal of Research and Practice,* 2000, 24(3), 219–233.
Western Association of Schools and Colleges Accrediting Commission for Community and Junior Colleges. *1996 Handbook of Accreditation and Policy Manual.* [http://www.accjsc.org/standard.htm]. 2000.
Western Association of Schools and Colleges Accrediting Commission for Senior Colleges and Universities. *Western Association of Schools and Colleges Draft Handbook of Accreditation 2000.* [http://www.wascweb.org/senior/handbook.html]. 2000.

DAWN GERONIMO TERKLA is executive director of institutional research and planning at Tufts University, Medford, Massachusetts.

7

Competency-based models that have been developed from pioneering work can be used to implement and refine programs at the institutional level. Lessons gained from these models can provide a foundation for institutional efforts to create models and can save valuable implementation time.

Creating and Implementing Competency-Based Learning Models

Alice Bedard Voorhees

Institutional accountability, articulation and student transfer issues, and workplace market alignment have become critical drivers that can provide the impetus for institutions to shift to competency-based models. As Karen Paulson notes earlier in this issue, business and industry have become vocal in their observation that students come to the workplace academically prepared yet often cannot apply these skills to workplace tasks. At the same time, the accountability movement traces its roots, at least in part, to the public's perception that most college graduates are lacking in the broader set of knowledge commonly known as general education. Implementing competency-based learning may not solve all known problems associated with documenting learning, but because they focus on performance and demonstrable outcomes, these models can serve as the building blocks for institutional actions to respond to the learning revolution.

The very mention of competency-based learning evokes a range of responses. Reasonable people may argue that total alignment with external demands for competencies may subvert the purposes of higher education. Still others may not agree on what parts of a student's total educational experience should be competency based. There can be no uniform answers to these concerns as institutions across higher education operate in many different environments and circumstances. The increased attention paid to competencies surfaces much of the ambivalence present in American higher education. Previous chapters have teased out many of these underlying issues in current delivery strategies. By now, these tensions should not be surprising to the reader. This chapter focuses on the pioneering work in

NEW DIRECTIONS FOR INSTITUTIONAL RESEARCH, no. 110, Summer 2001 © John Wiley & Sons, Inc.

competency learning models and their evaluation, which may save would-be implementers valuable time.

The models reviewed here represent well-developed thinking about the current state of competency-based learning. Institutional researchers can use these summaries to educate their colleagues about the possibilities inherent in competency-based learning models. Beyond informing constituencies about these models, institutional researchers can also aid their institutions by assisting with the evaluative efforts to implement these models. Meaningful evaluation starts with understanding the differences between the act of facilitating learning, as posed by these models, and the traditional, and frequently one-way, transmission of knowledge. Faculty evaluation also has its roots in the ability of the faculty to implement these models and to see their utility for their work.

General Education Models

Because of their sheer complexity, general education curricula are the least amenable to the possibilities posed by competency-based learning models. As Elizabeth Jones notes in Chapter Two, faculty in general education areas are often skeptical, if not resistant, to external efforts to shape or refine the curricula. General education is wider in content than specific disciplines and is marked by less general agreement about eventual outcomes. Since the 1960s, students have had a wide range of choices for meeting general education requirements. The result has been the implementation of curricular offerings that seek to expose learners to a myriad of concepts and discipline-based frameworks for learning. Attempts to reduce this sometimes bewildering collection of curricular offerings to measurable competencies can pose significant challenges for faculty and institutional researchers.

In contrast, faculty in programs that lead to professions or those whose curricula are closely aligned with business enjoy a more natural connection to competency-based learning models. These connections are based on the connections between student performance and eventual entry into occupations and professional roles. The uneven use of competencies throughout the entire undergraduate curriculum is common at most institutions. However, there is much at stake in implementing competency models throughout all institutional programs, including improving student movement within and through institutions. General education has much to say about the future of competency-based models and their implementation at most institutions.

Alverno College and Rutgers are widely recognized for their efforts to reform general education. Both institutions have decided what outcomes matter for liberal arts students. Alverno defines its curriculum in terms of the abilities that students need for effectiveness in the worlds of work, family, and civic community (www.alverno.edu). Alverno incorporates the practice of assessment with both course and multicourse assessment. The Alverno process requires reflective evaluation by the learner as a key dimension of assessment, a process known as *student assessment-as-learning*.

For institutions without a history in measuring general education, the best place to start is with institutionally developed statements regarding expectations for student learning. These statements can be found in most institutional catalogues and can serve as a touchstone for developing competency-based learning models. The process of updating these statements, particularly given the participation of a general education faculty, can serve as a springboard to competency implementation. The Rutgers and Alverno experiences created expectations that a liberally educated student can expect to demonstrate competency in four broad areas—higher-order cognitive skills, active awareness of one's natural environment, active awareness of oneself, and awareness of and effective action in one's social and cultural environment (Diamond, 1998).

Diamond points out how these expectations in general education might serve as a model for curricular development. First, although these expectations appear to be widely accepted, institutions might add or delete from the list to suit their circumstances. Second, institutions most certainly should decide what particular course content would serve to develop the larger competencies. Given this agreement, the actual authoring of accompanying competency statements should embrace clarity of language that recognizes the need for unambiguous assessment. Initial lack of measurement capacity, however, should not determine whether a competency should be written; measurement strategies can eventually be implemented. Finally, the sequencing of competencies within delivery of content is a critical decision that can serve as the necessary foundation for the success of model implementation.

Western Governors University (WGU) also provides a potential model for the delivery of competency-based general education. WGU's degree programs require demonstration of acquired competencies, not simply amassing course requirements. Rather than defining a degree by courses taken within a given area of study—such as the traditional areas of general education, major and minor requirements, and electives—WGU labels and organizes categories of competencies under the term *domains*. Some of these domains serve a group of degrees, and some are unique to a particular degree. Skill sets are further divided into subdomains. Each subdomain lists learning statements at some more granular level of performance objectives that students must master.

Spanning both professional and general education programs, WGU's approach seeks to provide multiple pathways for students to develop competencies for a given program or certificate. After initial assessment and advisement, WGU mentors assist students to develop learning plans and paths to the development of competencies under the domains developed for a given certificate or degree. The largest contribution of WGU to the academic community is its design of entire competency-defined degrees. Reflecting the best thinking about undergraduate education, these competencies were developed in conjunction with faculty, industry, and assessment experts from throughout the United States. These processes consisted of working meetings, discussions, and eventual refinements, especially in the general education area. Given the rigorous development of these competencies, it is difficult to imagine that a serious challenge might be mounted as to the validity of competencies in WGU's general education area. An accurate wording of the domains and competency statements is available on the WGU Web site (www.wgu.edu).

The Maricopa Community College District has created a large-scale model for linking competencies to curricula, with the goal of facilitating articulation among its own colleges in addition to four-year institutions. The close coordination of competencies with content outlines permits a full view of all skills developed by a particular course, including the lower-level skills that serve as the foundation for teaching subsequent higher-level skills (www.dist.maricopa.edu). The Maricopa model for curriculum development specifies that courses first be proposed at the campus level, where local needs are felt most strongly, and approved at the district level. There, a campus course facilitator, an instructional designer, and a faculty content specialist interact as a team to develop curriculum guides for each course. This site is an especially instructive guide for constructing a large-scale, systematic database to guide evolution to a competency-based model. Maricopa's leadership in competency-based learning is also evidenced by a second Web site, which contains competencies for programs created under the auspices of a National Science Foundation grant (see www.matec.org).

Trait-Based Scales. Trait-based scales and their scoring rubrics provide a valuable tool for reducing the ambiguity of competencies, especially the complex, higher-level competencies associated with general education. Institutions can also approach the assessment of general education and the continued development of program-specific higher-level competencies through the development of these scales and rubrics (Walvoord and Anderson, 1998). Scoring rubrics are descriptive scoring schemes and often appear as checklists, which are developed to guide and evaluate student learning. Commonly used to guide the evaluation of student writing samples, in which subjective judgments among faculty or other raters can sway evaluations of the quality of student work, scoring rubrics developed by experts specify the predefined level of observed quality, which can lend more objectivity to ranking. Useful examples of rubrics and sample rubrics can be found at the Illinois Online Network site, which is a partnership of forty-eight community colleges and the University of Illinois, Urbana (www.illinois.online.uillinois.edu/model/rubric.htm).

Although rubrics are used to produce agreement on student performance, their application is informed by the process of competency development, as trait-based scales evolve to measure particular learning competencies. For example, if a desired competency is for students to write a solidly coherent, structured narrative essay, a trait-based scoring rubric would define explicitly what observed characteristics would determine student success. Walvoord and Anderson (1998) offer practitioners a collection of trait-based scales that faculty from various disciplines have created. The relevancy of this work to competency-based discussions may be found in the surfacing of important curricular decisions based on the classroom-grading level. Competencies announce what the learner can expect to know or show as the result of learning. Accordingly, trait-based scales and scoring rubrics provide clear guidance to the learner as to how the professor is observing and rating specific learning behavior. These devices also provide consistency in processes that are often judged as subjective, providing a level of accountability for challenges by external audiences. Although the use of trait-based scales may require faculty training, consensus, and application, the development of trait-based scoring may likely surface existing skills among faculty who previously have been involved in other holistic-grading efforts.

Industry-Based Models

Recent progress in isolating competencies in general education and liberal arts areas is closely related to the institution's sense of academic tradition. In contrast, competencies that name what students will demonstrate by way of workplace attributes and profession-specific skills have long been part of career and technical, or vocational, college programs. These programs, particularly those funded by the Carl D. Perkins Vocational and Applied Technology and Vocational Education Act, now in its third iteration, have a twenty-plus-year history of setting program standards. The effect of these federal acts has been to increase visibility for competency standards, resulting in widespread acceptance of performance-based learning throughout both secondary and postsecondary career and technical programs (Parsad and Farris, 2000). Career and technical programs benefit directly from several national projects initiated over the past decade that have sought to develop and standardize competencies across occupations and the programs that prepare graduates to enter those occupations.

The use of SCANS 2000 (www.scans.jhu.edu) and the National Skills Standards Projects (www.nssb.org) has been illustrated by previous authors in this volume. Both projects are ambitious in scope. The focus of SCANS is on more general, transferable skills, whereas the National Skills Standards are more technically specific. Because the competencies developed are not aggregated in the same location, potential implementers need to check with both sites to ensure adequate coverage for their programs. These collections also represent great strides toward establishing a universal system for competencies. In practice, however, most career and technical programs are operated at local levels, where local decision makers determine program content. Even though local programs may be guided by national competency models and may result in a local or state-recognized occupational credential, except for those guided by national professional organizations, precious few will result in a nationally recognized credential. Consequently, for the majority of career and technical programs, the goal of full portability has yet to be achieved. A universal set of standards across all occupations will only result when all industries in a given sector, such as manufacturing, start to require standard competencies. This vision is further clouded when national standards for a professional organization or occupation are not endorsed by routine state approval processes. Finally, the future of universal standards may never be fully realized until trade associations, unions, and professional organizations themselves honor, or articulate, one another's competencies. Efforts to centrally locate these competencies would signify substantial agreement by professions and other occupational groups that in turn could lead to a "national work passport" for worker certification.

The future of portable employment skills in the building and construction trades is now being pursued by the Renaissance Project (2000). This is a joint education and industry venture among a range of public and private sector partners. The goal is a knowledge-based curriculum that utilizes national standards to produce a national workforce with portable skill sets. The attention to professional skills is also gaining ground in the professional associations, although these areas also incorporate competencies beyond those required for basal functioning. Accounting, for example, includes communication, problem solving, and analytical skills in its desired professional competencies for the CPA exam (www.icpas.org/icpas/educator/comexam.htm).

Librarians of specialized collections also advocate their desired competencies on the Internet (www.jenkinslaw.org/research/librarians/competencies.shtml), as do professional trainers through the International Board for Training Performance and Instruction (www.ibstpi.org). Propagating these competencies affects the very structure of job positions and resulting training menus for these organizations. Again, such standards are not universal for either librarians or trainers at this point. Whether competencies are voluntary or mandatory across professional organizations, there is no single source or directory that centralizes these efforts. Ownership issues, and perhaps the newness of these Web sites, have resulted in separateness. Aggregation of these competencies at the National Skills Standards Board site, for instance, would be a valuable contribution to efforts to promote national skills.

The value of competency-based learning models is not limited to their application to current students. Those already employed, often termed *incum-*

bent workers, in business and industry are a large and mostly untapped market for most institutions. A captive audience is likely to be motivated to quickly learn specific skills in their jobs that may lead to advancement. Incumbent workers need specific learning opportunities delivered in expedient ways and at times that are convenient to the employee and the employer. An incumbent worker may not be so much degree seeking as interested in learning for current workplace goals. It is here that the work spent in developing competency-based models and the resulting ability to assemble specific content for delivery will pay a large premium.

The Community Colleges of Colorado have created a performance-based curriculum model for the retrieval and customization of curriculum for workforce learning to address the needs of incumbent workers (U.S. Department of Education, 2001). This center has created competency-based learning modules in partnerships between training divisions of community colleges and large employers. Utilizing standardized formats for naming and assessing competencies, the modules created under this project can be combined with other learning opportunities or can be delivered by themselves directly to learners (www.coloradotraining.org). This project is currently exploring the connections between training content, technical program skills standards, and competency-defined college courses.

Implementing Competency-Based Learning Models

The availability and ease of access to competency-based learning models do not, by themselves, ensure successful implementation. Even if one begins with the premise that all competencies delivered are reliable and valid, evaluation of the effectiveness of these efforts clearly is new ground. In fact, the Jones, Voorhees, and Paulson study (U.S. Department of Education, 2001) found that few early implementers of competency-based learning models have formal processes in place for assessing the reliability and validity of their competencies. Instead, the considerable effort expended by these cutting-edge projects has been directed toward delivery processes, not to formal evaluation schemes. This should come as no surprise because the traditional delivery of instruction, focusing on teacher performance as opposed to learner performance, is in some ways easier to evaluate than competency-based models. The level of granularity inherent in competency-based learning models also increases the potential number of measurements that must be created and validated.

Faculty are integral to the evaluation of competency-based learning, as they ideally are involved in conceptualizing, defining, delivering, and assessing competencies. O'Banion (2000) refers to the critical need to train whole faculties in order to accomplish the shift from teacher-centered to learner-centered paradigms. The past ten years have witnessed many institutions using the term *learner centered* to describe their fundamental missions. Competency-based models enjoy an obvious connection to aspirational student learning statements because they shift the focus from instructional delivery to student performance. The ability to evaluate these programs depends in no small way on the ability of faculty to engage in new delivery paradigms. Virtually no course work exists within graduate discipline programs to prepare scholar-experts in either the basics of traditional pedagogy or applied assessment. Less than 30 percent of general education faculty in a national survey report using scholarly sources on teaching and learning for planning their courses and developing syllabi (Stark and Latucca, cited in Diamond, 1998, p. xv). Engagement in learner-centered paradigms carries the obligation to shift away from unexamined assumptions about learning, which result in pedagogy that lacks adequate assessment and evidence, and toward an approach that applies relevant knowledge to improve practice (Angelo, 1996). Angelo and Patricia Cross have developed an inventory, the Teaching Goals Inventory: Self-Scoreable Version, that helps faculty identify their instructional goals in quantifiable ways so that they can assess their delivery. This instrument can be used to support the transformation of teaching and evaluation (Diamond, 1998). Providing clear demarcation between teaching and learning goals, this inventory can assist faculty in thinking about their teaching behavior and the results they seek.

The Wisconsin Technical College System responded to the need to educate faculty about the use of competencies and to create a consistent statewide curriculum by creating instructional design software known as the Wisconsin Instructional Design System (WIDS, see www.wids.org). A course was also designed to certify faculty in the use of the software. WIDS provides the structure for guiding a faculty, from taking standards and breaking them into task levels through the purposeful construction of instructional objectives and assessment items. The theoretical basis for using the software still requires that faculty understand Bloom's taxonomy (Bloom and others, 1956). The use of the software embeds a common structure to the definition of courses throughout the system that uses it. The roots of WIDS can be directly traced to the technical education area. Accordingly, subject specialists from these areas may be more comfortable with its level of detail than liberal arts faculty.

In some cases, instructional designers also assist faculty subject experts in creating a fully developed competency-based course or program. Evaluation of competency-based programs cannot be exclusively the province of faculty, however. Many parts of the institution need to collaborate to effectively implement these models and to subsequently evaluate their success. Drawing from the professional experience of implementers of competency-based programs and the informed principles of strong practice contained in a recent National Postsecondary Education Cooperative working group study on competencies (U.S. Department of Education, 2001), Exhibit 7.1 presents a framework for these criteria.

Exhibit 7.1. A Checklist for Evaluating Competency-Based Models

Faculty Preparation

Have faculty been oriented to the shift from teacher-centered delivery to student-centered performance?

Have faculty been involved in conceptualizing, identifying, and delivering program competencies?

Have faculty received training in writing competency statements that are measurable?

Do faculty understand the levels of cognitive mastery expressed by Bloom's Taxonomy?

Can faculty implement classroom assessment techniques to evaluate student learning?

Model Preparation

Does the model relate to and further the institution's stated mission?

How do industry-related competencies draw from state and national standards and credentials?

Are all competencies assessable?

What provisions are there within the model to ensure that competencies are valid and reliable?

Are the assessments for competencies valid and reliable?

Does the institution have a publicized statement on expectations for student learning? If so, are competencies aligned with that statement?

What is the life cycle of competencies within the model? Is there a replacement schedule that aligns with new developments in knowledge or career areas?

Student Advisement

How are learners trained or oriented to the competency-based paradigm?

Are learners made aware of how they may import their preexisting competencies into the model?

Administration

Is there commitment at the top of the organization to the model?

Are adequate resources available to implement and sustain the model?

How will competencies be recorded?

What steps have been taken with other organizations and entities to ensure that competencies are portable?

What mechanisms are in place for formative evaluation? For summative evaluation?

Source: Some data are from U.S. Department of Education, 2001.

Annotated Web Bibliography

Alverno College. "Ability-Based Curriculum." [www.alverno.edu/educators].
    This site provides an overview of Alverno's theory and practice of performance-based assessment of student learning as well as its approach

to program and institutional assessment of learning outcomes. This site is useful for practitioners wanting a wide view of one institution's twenty-plus-years' experience in competency-based models.

American Association for Higher Education. "Nine Principles of Good Practice for Assessing Student Learning." [www.aahe.org/principl.htm].

A touchstone for institutions and programs wishing to implement or refine their existing competency-based efforts, this site provides criteria from which to evaluate successful practice.

America's Learning Exchange (ALX) Guide to Workforce Assessment. [www.alx.org/testass.asp].

ALX is a Web-based service sponsored by the U.S. Department of Labor and is supported by many professional training and educational organizations. The purpose of ALX is to provide a conduit for information about and access to education and training resources and to create an electronic marketplace for those resources. The testing and assessment page provides the public with a mechanism for viewing the licensure and certification requirements for various occupations and the corresponding assessments used for entry into those occupations.

Competencies for Certified Public Accountants. [http://www.icpas.org/icpas /educator/c-study.htm] and [http://www.icpas.org/icpas/educator/comexam.htm].

The first site makes recommendations for additional competencies needed by new CPAs. The second one examines issues in on-line delivery of the CPA exam.

Core Competencies for Specialized Librarians. [http://www.jenkinslaw.org /research/librarians/competencies.shtml].

This site contains links to competencies for library specializations in law library support, technical services, and technology competencies. It provides an overview of profession-specific competencies.

Downes, Stephen. "The Future of Online Learning." [http://www.atl.ualberta .ca/downes/future/home.html].

Downes is a visionary thinker who is well connected to technology and its implications for student access to learning via competencies. This report includes an overview of the decomposition of course content and technological options for creating new learning experiences.

Illinois Online Network. (sample rubrics) [http://illinois.online.uillinois .edu/model/rubric.htm].

This Web page provides several sample rubrics or checklists of characteristics that facilitate assessment of the quality of a learning product.

International Board of Standards for Training and Performance. [http://www .ibstpi.org].

This site details competencies for training managers, training instructors, and instructional designers. These competencies can be a useful resource for individuals and institutions wishing to compare and contrast their skills in creating competency-based models and in delivering those models.

Maricopa College District. [http://www.dist.maricopa.edu/eddev/artic].

This site is an example of a comprehensive course management system with crosswalks to competencies. There are separate pages for transfer and articulation, curriculum management, and learning and instruction. Course competencies are linked on this page.

National Organization for Competency Assurance (NOCA)/National Commission for Certifying Agencies (NCCA). [http://www.noca.org].

This site provides an overview of NOCA, an umbrella entity that develops standards and accredits certification organizations that meet them. The National Commission for Certifying Agencies (NCCA) is the accreditation body of NOCA and is the only national accreditation body for private certification organizations. NOCA membership includes the Advanced Certified Fund Raising Executive Program to the Society of Actuaries. This site is useful for examining the wide range of educational organizations that fall outside of the purview of regional accrediting bodies.

National Skills Standards Board. [http://www.nssb.org].

The NSSB is a voluntary national system of skill standards, assessment and certification systems whose purpose is to enhance the ability of the U.S. workforce to compete effectively in a global economy. This site provides over thirty industry skill standards, ranging from advanced high-performance manufacturing to human services to retail trade.

North Carolina State University Internet Resources for Higher Education Outcomes Assessment. [http://www2.acs.ncsu.edu/UPA/assmt/resource.htm].

This site is a collection of assessment-related links and contains many examples of institutional outcomes assessment programs.

Paulson, Karen. "Annotated Bibliography." In U.S. Department of Education, National Center for Education Statistics. *Defining and Assessing Learning: Exploring Competency-Based Initiatives.* Washington, D.C.: U.S. Department of Education, 2001. [http://nces.ed.gov/npec/products.html].

This is an annotated bibliography that was prepared for the Data Ramifications of Competency-Based Initiatives Work Group, National Postsecondary Education Cooperative. This is an excellent source for examining the relevant literature on competencies.

SCANS 2000. [http://www.scans.jhu.edu].

This site is an access point to the Secretary's Commission on Achieving Necessary Skills (SCANS) project and is now housed at The Johns Hopkins University. It contains an overview of the career transcript system as well as links to SCANS and assessment.

SUCCEED Coalition of Engineering Schools. [http://www.succeed.vt.edu].

SUCCEED is one of several National Science Foundation–sponsored coalitions of engineering colleges committed to a comprehensive revitalization of undergraduate engineering education. This site is an example of collaborative thinking about the competencies that should constitute future delivery strategies. This effort parallels the National Skills Standards Board.

Western Governors University Degree with Industry certification. [www.wgu.edu/wgu/academics/cne_listing.html].

This provides an overview of the competency-based associate of applied science degree in information technology–certified network engineering. This is an example of embedding industry certification in a degree program.

Wisconsin Instructional Design Software. [http://www.wids.org/default.asp].

The Wisconsin Technical College System created Wisconsin instructional design software (WIDS) to assist faculty to create competency-based courses based on industry standards.

Wisconsin's ASE Automotive Technician Degree and Credential. [http://www.blackhawk.tec.wi.us/programs/techdiplo/autotech.htm].

This vocational degree also embeds industry certification.

References

Angelo, T. A. "Developing Learning Communities and Seven Promising Shifts and Seven Powerful Levers." Paper presented at a meeting of the Professional and Organizational Development Network in Higher Education, Salt Lake City, Utah, 1996.

Bloom, B. S., and others. *Taxonomy of Educational Objectives. Handbook I: Cognitive Domain.* New York: McKay, 1956.

Diamond, R. M. *Designing and Assessing Courses and Curricula: A Practical Guide.* (Rev. ed.) San Francisco: Jossey-Bass, 1998.

O'Banion, T. "An Inventory for Learning-Centered Colleges." *Community College Journal,* 2000, 71(1) 14–23.

Parsad, B., and Farris, E. *Occupational Programs and the Use of Skills and Competencies at the Secondary and Postsecondary Levels, 1999.* National Center for Education Statistics report no. 2000-23. Washington, D.C.: U.S. Department of Education, Office of Educational Research and Improvement, Feb. 2000.

Renaissance Project. "America's Community Colleges Working Together for Building and Construction Trades Education." Paper presented at the National Conference for Occupational Education, Westminster, Colo., Oct. 2000.

U.S. Department of Education, National Center for Education Statistics. *Defining and Assessing Learning: Exploring Competency-Based Initiatives* (by E. Jones, R. A. Voorhees, and K. Paulson for the Council of the National Postsecondary Education Cooperative Competency-Based Initiatives Working Group). Washington, D.C.: U.S. Department of Education, National Center for Education Statistics, 2001.

Walvoord, B. E., and Anderson, V. J. *Effective Grading: A Tool for Learning and Assessment.* San Francisco: Jossey-Bass, 1998.

ALICE BEDARD VOORHEES is director of curriculum and instruction for the Community Colleges of Colorado System.

8

This bibliography is for those interested in using competencies as an alternative to more traditional measures of student achievement in postsecondary education. It is not meant to be exhaustive; rather, it is illustrative of the many works available about competencies—their definition, measurement, and use.

An Annotated Bibliography on Competencies

Karen Paulson

Competencies, as used in this bibliography, refer to specific statements of student performance in terms of skills, knowledge, and abilities. Several questions guided the choice of articles, books, and monographs to be included. First and foremost, were competencies explicitly used? Was there an explicit statement of or attempt to grapple with student competence? How were those explicit competency statements used in the processes of the activity? How were competencies documented? How were competencies particularly useful in the transition from one activity to another?

Because of taking this approach, certain bodies of literature were not included in order to keep the bibliography manageable—for instance, there are large literatures on performance indicators, performance funding, accountability, and assessment that were omitted. The number of institutional examples was limited as well in order to focus on the use of competencies in larger processes. The constraint of not giving too many individual institutional citations curtailed the number of practical examples given because many institutions document narrowly and do not contain guidelines on how to adapt approaches to a variety of institutional settings.

Many possibilities of specific occupational and industry-specific competency lists that have been compiled by various groups have not been included. For those interested, a few suggested starting points are the National Skills Standards Board Web site (www.nssb.org), which includes links to state skill standards sites; the Occupational Skills Standards Projects

This bibliography first appeared in a report of the National Postsecondary Education Cooperative Competency-Based Initiatives Working Group (U.S. Department of Education, 2001).

(www.ed.gov/offices/OVAE/OccSkills/index.html); the School-to-Work Internet Gateway (www.stw.ed.gov); the Secretary's Commission on Achieving Necessary Skills site at Johns Hopkins University (www.scans.jhu.edu /default.htm); O*NET, the Occupational Information Network (www.doleta .gov/programs/onet/onet_hp.htm); and the National Center on Education and the Economy (www.ncee.org). Other occupational and industry-specific competency lists appear throughout this volume, especially in the Web bibliography prepared by Alice Bedard Voorhees for her chapter.

This bibliography is composed of five sections. The first is a general introduction to the history and basics of competencies in postsecondary education. The second contains citations about entry into postsecondary education, including competency-based admissions and placement. The third section focuses on the use of competencies within postsecondary education, such as competency-based curricula, general education competencies, and transfer competencies both within and across providers. Exit from postsecondary education, including end-of-program competencies, those used for employment placement and for admittance to graduate or professional schools, are found in the fourth section. Finally, the fifth section is about the use of competencies for overall institutional effectiveness, including program improvement, accountability, performance budgeting, and accreditation.

Section I. General Introduction to Competencies in Postsecondary Education

This section is included for the novice, one who is in need of a general introduction to the use of competencies in postsecondary education. Included here are basic materials about the construction of competencies as well as the historical development of the use of competencies.

Basics of Competencies

Mager, R. F. *Preparing Instructional Objectives: A Critical Tool in the Development of Effective Instruction.* (3rd ed.) Atlanta: Center for Effective Performance, 1997.

Mager is considered one of the leading experts on instructional objectives. This is a straightforward "how-to" book on constructing usable instructional objectives (competencies). The strength of Mager's approach comes from its applicability to both education and corporate-training situations. His book is written with a broad, accessible perspective.

Parry, S. B. "Just What Is a Competency? (And Why Should You Care?)" *Training,* June 1998, pp. 58–64.

This article gives a business- and training-oriented perspective about the important differences between competencies and traits or characteristics, skills and abilities, as well as between competencies, styles, and values. For

Parry, competencies are generic, limited to ten to fourteen per company, and how individuals act them out is dependent largely on personality ("style/ values"). Assessment techniques advocated include 360-degree feedback, role playing in a controlled laboratory situation, and the use of interactive media.

Walvoord, B. E., and Anderson, V. J. *Effective Grading: A Tool for Learning and Assessment.* San Francisco: Jossey-Bass, 1998.

Walvoord and Anderson's book is about making explicit the criteria used in grading. Of particular interest are Chapter Five, "Establishing Criteria and Standards for Grading," and Appendix C, "Examples of Primary Trait-Based Scales Developed by Faculty." These are useful because of the explicitness necessary when writing competency statements and when agreeing on the criteria used to evaluate competence. Although these pages focus on a specific technique, *primary trait analysis,* the principles and processes are useful when working with competencies.

Historical Background of Competencies

Grant, G., and Associates. *On Competence: A Critical Analysis of Competence-Based Reforms in Higher Education.* San Francisco: Jossey-Bass, 1979.

This volume is one of the only available that has as its subjects *both* competency and higher education; most of the other general books on competency-based education noted in this bibliography are about elementary and secondary education. A definition that is of value now is offered early in the book, "Competence-based education tends to be a form of education that derives a curriculum from an analysis of a prospective or actual role in modern society and that attempts to certify student progress on the basis of demonstrated performance in some or all aspects of that role. Theoretically, such demonstrations of competence are independent of time served in formal educational settings" (p. 6). Of particular note are the chapters by David Riesman, "Society's Demands for Competence," and Thomas Ewen's "Analyzing the Impact of Competence-Based Approaches on Liberal Education." Riesman gives a historical summary of societal forces and why they resulted in competency-based education. Ewen grapples with the ever-present tension between the concepts of liberal education and competence.

Doll, W. E., Jr. "Developing Competence." In E. C. Short (ed.), *Competence: Inquiries into Its Meaning and Acquisition in Educational Settings.* Lanham, Md.: University Press of America, 1984.

Urch, G. E. "A Philosophical Perspective on Competency Based Education." In R. T. Utz and L. D. Leonard (eds.), *The Foundations of Competency Based Education.* Dubuque, Iowa: Kendall/Hunt, 1975.

These two chapters are for those who are interested in the philosophical background of competency-based education. They are from the 1970s but remain salient. Doll distinguishes *competence* and its relationship to *performance* based on Chomsky, Piaget, and Bruner. Urch cites critics, including Neill, Goodman, Rogers, and Illich, and then traces the "roots" of competency-based education back to rationalism (Descartes and Spinoza), empiricism (Bacon, Locke, Herbart, and Thorndike), pragmatism (Dewey), and behaviorism (Skinner and Gagne).

Klemp, G. O., Jr. "Identifying, Measuring, and Integrating Competence." In P. S. Pottinger and J. Goldsmith (eds.), *Defining and Measuring Competence.* New Directions for Experiential Learning, no. 3. San Francisco: Jossey-Bass, 1979.

This chapter from a late 1970s volume contains a useful discussion about the definition of competence, the interaction of competence and performance, and the integration of competencies. Klemp also discusses responses to testing for competence, illustrating the problems with traditional testing, and suggests "intermediate criteria" for grading—efficiency, parsimony, thoroughness, and outcome effectiveness. He acknowledges that there is no one right answer, "A wide range of permissible responses helps prevent 'ceiling' and 'floor' effects that restrict the useful range of competency measurement" (p. 48).

Section II. Competencies for Entry into Postsecondary Education

Citations in this section of the bibliography are about the use of competencies in the undergraduate admissions process. The other topic pertinent to this section is placement examination. However, very little has been written about the use of competencies for use in collegiate placement examination. Although some assessments and testing products are based on competencies (such as the Regents Examinations, New Standards, and the American College Testing [ACT] Program's Work Keys), there is little documentation of their use in postsecondary education, either specifically as placement examinations or because of their focus on competencies.

Conley, D. T. "Daddy, I'm Scared: A Prophetic Parable." *Phi Delta Kappan,* 1996, 78(4), 290–297.

Conley, D. T. "Where's Waldo? The Conspicuous Absence of Higher Education from School Reform and One State's Response." *Phi Delta Kappan,* 1996, 78(4), 309–314.

These two articles by Conley are about the Proficiency-Based Admission Standards System (PASS) Project in Oregon. PASS is a high school graduation–college admission system based on proficiencies (competencies). The "prophetic parable" article is about the context PASS operates in, how they determined the proficiency standards, and how Conley believes those standards will force higher education to change, particularly with regard to admission requirements. "Where's Waldo?" focuses on how the PASS project fits into statewide education reform across the K–16 continuum. A balanced appraisal is given of opportunities and obstacles. (See also the PASS Web site: www.pass-us.uoregon.edu/info.)

Conley, D. *Statewide Strategies for Implementing Competency-Based Admissions Standards.* [www.sheeo.org/SHEEO/pubs-strategy-brief-admissions.htm]. Jan. 1999.

Conley summarizes the results of a survey and case studies done by the State Higher Education Executive Officers organization regarding competency-based admissions. These systems are defined as "requir[ing] students to demonstrate their knowledge and skills in specified academic areas and at specified performance levels." Eleven states replied affirmatively that they were considering or implementing competency-based admissions systems. Six states (Colorado, Georgia, Maryland, Ohio, Washington, and Wisconsin) were chosen for additional study. The document includes a discussion of the policy context and reasons for considering a competency model; a short overview of the development, implementation, and assessment of competencies; what the results have been so far in these states; and what the continuing problems are in the conversion to such systems. Conley notes that whether these competency-based systems work "better" than traditional admissions systems is being closely watched.

Roberts, R., and Robson, R. *Electronic Transcripts in the Age of Standards.* [pass-ous.oregon.edu/info/staff/roberts/electronic_transcripts.html]. 1998.

This is a short overview of how electronic transcripts are specified and will be constructed for use with the Oregon PASS system. They contain three levels of data. The first is "summative scores or binary decisions" regarding a student's achievement. The second level will be "verifications" of these decisions and will consist of who made the decision, what it was based on, and when the decision was made. The third level is the actual work on which the student's achievement level is based.

Sills-Briegel, T., Fisk, C., and Dunlop, V. "Graduation by Exhibition," *Education Leadership,* 1996, *54*(4), 66–71.

This article is an example of how competencies are documented and assessed as a high school graduation requirement. This requirement—an individual thesis project—uses a committee of three overseers to work with each student. The committee is composed of one instructor randomly assigned to the student and two people of the student's choice (one often comes from outside the high school, either a member of the community or someone from a local university). Levels of achievement are "not proficient," "proficient," and "distinguished performance." Criteria used to evaluate the projects include personal responsibility, critical thinking, writing, public speaking, and multimedia presentation. No indication is given as to how graduates use these projects either as supporting evidence for college admission or for job attainment.

University of Wisconsin System. *Final Report: The University of Wisconsin System Competency-Based Admission Pilot Project.* [www.uwsa.edu/acadaff /cba/report.htm]. Spring 1998.

In 1992, the University of Wisconsin began studying competency-based admissions as an alternative to traditional admissions for those students attending high schools with nontraditional curricula. It is now an option available to students, although it is never meant to replace the existing admissions system. The final report is useful because it contains data comparing traditional admissions measures (ACT and grades) with the new competency-based admissions measures as well as data on the retention of students admitted using the competency-based approach. Measures of time put into the admissions decisions by university personnel and a sample admissions reporting profile are also given.

Section III. Competencies within Postsecondary Education

This section highlights the use of competencies within postsecondary education. Competencies may be used in a variety of ways, including as curricular guides, as a means of validating experiential education and knowledge learned outside a formal educational setting, for specifying and easing articulation and transfer, and as feedback for students regarding their progress and learning expectations.

Experiential Education

Lamdin, L. *Earn College Credit for What You Know.* (2nd ed.) Chicago: Council for Adult and Experiential Learning, 1992.

Whitaker, U. *Assessing Learning: Standards, Principles, and Procedures.* Philadelphia: Council for Adult and Experiential Learning, 1989.

Although both books are written from the perspective of awarding credits (due primarily to the prevalent academic climate when they were first published), the standards proposed and the information given are applicable to competency-based processes and projects. Whitaker outlines and explains the standards for *prior learning assessment* as designed by the Council for Adult and Experiential Learning. Lamdin affirms the many nonacademic, nonclassroom methods of learning.

General Education

Alverno College Faculty. *Student Assessment-as-Learning at Alverno College.* (3rd ed.) Milwaukee, Wis.: Alverno College, 1994.

Farmer, D. W. *Enhancing Student Learning: Emphasizing Essential Competencies in Academic Programs.* Wilkes-Barre, Pa.: King's College, 1988.

Both Alverno College in Wisconsin (www.alverno.edu) and Kings College in Pennsylvania (www.kings.edu) were early postsecondary innovators, incorporating core competencies into their curricula over twenty years ago. Alverno's faculty restructured their institution around eight abilities that each student should have: communication ability, analysis, problem solving, valuing in decision making, social interaction, global perspectives, effective citizenship, and aesthetic responsiveness. They couple their focus on abilities with student assessment that is authentic and reality based. King's College came to large-scale curriculum reform as a result of working on a planning project. In their CORE curriculum taken by all students, they seek to instill the skills of liberal learning: critical thinking, effective writing, effective oral communication, library and information literacy, computer competence, creative thinking and problem solving, quantitative reasoning, and moral reasoning. Farmer presents a thorough description of the hurdles as well as the benefits of the new approach.

Jones, E. A. (ed.). *Preparing Competent College Graduates: Setting New and Higher Expectations for Student Learning.* New Directions for Higher Education, no. 96. San Francisco: Jossey-Bass, 1996.

Jones gives a summary of the recent press for "competent" college graduates in the first chapter of this volume. Subsequent chapters are devoted to comprehensive reviews regarding what competencies are generally agreed on in speech communication and listening, effective writing, critical reading, and problem solving.

Career and Professional Education

Gonczi, A. "Competency Based Assessment in the Professions in Australia." *Assessment in Education,* 1994, 1(1), 27–44.

This article is a good introduction to the entire competency assessment process. The section included on policy issues is comprehensive, focusing primarily on asking questions, not necessarily answering them. Two case studies included in the article give real-world examples of competencies, how they were assessed, and what the criteria were for evaluation of assessment results. These are good, practical, and short examples of implementation.

Competency-Based Curricula

Sinclair Community College. *Continuous Improvement Through the Assessment of Student Learning Outcomes: A Work in Progress: Department Assessment Reviews and Program Learning Outcomes.* Dayton, Ohio: Sinclair Community College, June 1998.

Sinclair Community College is a good example of an institution whose faculty have grappled with how to determine student learning outcomes. For each department, the document lists the guidelines and existing outcome lists referenced, student learning outcomes for the department, a cross-listing of those outcomes with existing courses, assessment methods, the results of assessments, what institutional and departmental action has been taken based on those results, and perspectives on general education and overall outcomes.

Western Governors University. *A Proposed "Academic Infrastructure" for Credentialing at the Western Governors University (WGU).* Draft. [www.wgu.edu /wgu/about/acad_infra.html]. Accessed Apr. 20, 2001.

This working document was used in the early stages of developing WGU. It gives the original conceptualization of the competency-based credentials offered by the institution and discusses the implications for practice in terms of the structure of the institution, staffing requirements, and the way that students would progress through WGU programs to successful degree completion.

Student Information on Expectations and Educational Progress

Banta, T. W., and Associates. *Making a Difference: Outcomes of a Decade of Assessment in Higher Education.* San Francisco: Jossey-Bass, 1993.

Banta, T. W., Lund, J. P., Black, K. E., and Oblander, F. W. *Assessment in Practice: Putting Principles to Work on College Campuses.* San Francisco: Jossey-Bass, 1996.

These two books by Banta and colleagues are compilations of institutional assessment programs; some of these programs are based on student demonstration of competence. In *Assessment in Practice,* each major heading (such as "Assessing Student Achievement in the Major") begins with a "chapter guide," which lists the assessment programs contained in the chapter "by institution, by subject area, by assessment method, and by case strengths." These volumes are good for identifying institutions that either currently use competencies or might have tried and decided against the use of competencies in their educational programs. In addition, *assessment centers* are often used in the documentation of student competence; in *Making a Difference,* Chapter Fifteen is devoted to assessment centers, including the pros and cons of such an approach.

Meade, J. "A Solution for Competency-Based Employee Development." *HRMagazine,* Dec. 1998, pp. 54–58.

This product review for a human resources magazine highlights a software package that tracks employees' competencies, monitors how those competencies match job requirements, provides links to available on-line training materials, and shows whether employees are making progress in their training for the competencies. Postsecondary institutions might start documentation of student competency with something similar.

Section IV. Competencies for Exit from Postsecondary Education

Workforce skills are the primary focus of the competencies used for exit from postsecondary education. This section includes citations on basic and workforce skills, performance certification, ways to match individual skills with particular job requirements, and the skills necessary for admission to and success in professional fields.

Basic Skills

Comprehensive Adult Student Assessment System (CASAS). *Extending the Ladder: From CASAS to Work Keys Assessments: Executive Summary.* [www.nifl.gov/CASAS-ACT.html]. 1997.

This executive summary offers the results of a study done that linked two systems—CASAS' Workforce Learning Systems, a basic adult literacy assessment system, and Work Keys, an assessment of employability skills. The article has a profile of the two systems, which includes examples of the assessment criteria used in both and practical descriptions of how the two systems are meshed together (the *extension ladder effect*). This overlap of systems allows them to collectively address a broader range of competence. This increased range provides a service to individuals who enter the basic literacy system and need to articulate to a more advanced skill level. Both systems use "'real-life' workforce tasks, as opposed to academic tasks." The study used data from 494 individuals who were randomly selected from twenty-seven sites in eight states. The authors conclude that Workforce Learning Systems is suitable for basic skill levels, that the midlevel of skills are addressed by either system, and that higher skill levels are best assessed using Work Keys. (See also ACT's *Work Keys Targets for Instruction.* Iowa City: American College Testing Program, 1994. Books are available in the following subject areas: writing, applied mathematics, teamwork, observation, locating information, listening, applied technology, and reading for information.)

Certification of Performance

Browning, A. H., Bugbee A. C., Jr., and Mullins, M. A. (eds.). *Certification: A NOCA Handbook.* Washington, D.C.: National Organization for Competency Assurance, 1996.

This volume is an excellent introduction to certification. Of particular interest to those interested in competency-based initiatives are the chapters

"Job Analysis" (Chapter Two), "Standard Setting" (Chapter Five), and "Future Trends in Credentialing" (Chapter Nine). Chapter Two provides a clear and unambiguous description of how to decompose a job into various tasks. The chapter on standard setting outlines the various theories of establishing standards for performance and methods for arriving at those standards.

Pottinger, P. S. "Competence Assessment: Comments on Current Practices." In P. S. Pottinger and J. Goldsmith (eds.), *Defining and Measuring Competence*. New Directions for Experiential Learning, no. 3. San Francisco: Jossey-Bass, 1979.

This chapter from the late 1970s focuses on licensing and registration based on demonstration of professional competence. It gives a short background introduction to professional competence and foreshadows many of the problems that continue to arise today, such as the reductionism inherent in long lists of behaviors and the need for multiple exemplars of competence.

Matching Skills and Job Requirements

Resnick, L. B., and Wirt, J. G. (eds.). *Linking School and Work: Roles for Standards and Assessment*. San Francisco: Jossey-Bass, 1996.

Resnick and Wirt's volume is based primarily on SCANS and New Standards work. For the purposes of this bibliography, the most important section is Part One, "Standards-Based Education for Workplace Readiness." The four chapters contained here are all useful, especially John H. Bishop's chapter on "Signaling the Competencies of High School Students to Employers," because it is a practical approach to linking competencies with seeking employment.

Professional Education

Curry, L., Wergin, J. F., and Associates. *Educating Professionals: Responding to New Expectations for Competence and Accountability*. San Francisco: Jossey-Bass, 1993.

Stark, J. S., Lowther, M. A., and Hagerty, B.M.K. *Responsive Professional Education: Balancing Outcomes and Opportunities*. ASHE-ERIC Higher Education Report no. 3. Washington, D.C.: Association for the Study of Higher Education, 1986.

Stark, Lowther, and Hagerty's monograph from the 1980s documents the results of an extensive literature review. From their review, the authors identified six professional competencies—conceptual competence, technical competence, contextual competence, interpersonal competence, integrative competence, and adaptive competence—and five professional attitudes—career marketability, professional identity, ethical standards, scholarly concern for improvement, and motivation for continued learning. Curry, Wergin, and their associates build on the work of Stark and her colleagues in their 1993 volume elaborating on the concept of professional competency. The first section sets the stage for the renewed urgency for competencies. The second section highlights how competencies allow distinctions to be made in professional education for the following: linking to actual practice, liberal learning, ethics, and critical thinking and problem solving. The third and final section discusses areas of praxis for the intelligent use of professional competencies in the twenty-first century.

Hagedorn, L. S., and Nora, A. "Rethinking Admissions Criteria in Graduate and Professional Programs." In J. G. Haworth (ed.), *Assessing Graduate and Professional Education: Current Realities, Future Prospects.* New Directions for Institutional Research, no. 92. San Francisco: Jossey-Bass, 1996.

This chapter is a quick summary of graduate admissions procedures, including a discussion of alternatives. Hagedorn and Nora highlight Stark, Lowther, and Hagerty's study of professional competence and ask the question, "How can [these competencies] be predicted?" Their conclusion is that more complex measures, such as writing samples, plans for research, and structured interviews, are necessary for determining graduate admission, but they do not go so far as to articulate admissions competencies. In a search to find institutions that use alternative forms of admissions criteria, only a handful of institutions could be identified. In those institutions, the departments using alternative criteria were primarily in the social sciences. These techniques included differential weighting of factors, portfolios, two-tier admissions processes (two on-site visits), and group interviews.

Workforce Development and Vocational Education

Evers, F. T., Rush, J. C., and Berdrow, I. *The Bases of Competence: Skills for Lifelong Learning and Employability.* San Francisco: Jossey-Bass, 1998.

This book pulls together a number of issues not previously covered in a single volume. The first part is about "Understanding Competence" and includes chapters on "the humbling effect" that occurs when recent college graduates or new employees realize that they are unable to apply what they learned at college. The second chapter offers a common language for use with competencies. Part Two outlines the four "Essential Skills and Competencies" that Evers, Rush, and Berdrow have identified—managing self, communicating, managing people and tasks, and mobilizing innovation and change. Part Three is the useful essence of this book, "Developing Competence." Three chapters explain how the transition from college to workplace needs attention from both academics and businesspeople, how colleges should be vigilant in their competency-based curricula and courses, and finally how employers can be alert to the effects of their organizational interactions with recent graduates as well as their partnerships with postsecondary education institutions. Part Four consists of three case studies, which illustrate the principles outlined in the earlier sections.

Packer, A. "The End of Routine Work and the Need for a Career Transcript." Paper presented at the Hudson Institute's Workforce 2020 Conference, Oct. 7, 1998. [www.scans.jhu.edu/CTS.html].

Packer discusses shifts in the match between the skills that employees bring and the skills necessary for meaningful, high-paid work in the future economy. He then links this to the educational challenges created by these skill shifts. Finally, he suggests the structure of a "career transcript," which is to "provide employers with *readable, comprehensible, believable, timely and convenient documents* [emphasis in original] that will help them choose the right applicant for the job." The career transcript would include standardized tests, workplace performance assessments, and "structured assessment of classroom performance on *benchmarked classroom tasks* [emphasis in original]," although presumably, based on his earlier arguments, "classroom" is not a necessary component of this latter requirement.

Stecher, B. M., Rahn, M. L., Ruby, A., Alt, M. N., and Robyn, A. *Using Alternative Assessments in Vocational Education*. Santa Monica, Calif.: RAND, 1997.

Stecher and colleagues write about vocational education that uses assessments to improve learning and instruction, certify individual mastery, and evaluate program success. They recognize that changes have occurred in vocational education, resulting in a broader continuum of skills, which range from general workplace skills to very specific occupational skills. They point out that to evaluate skill acquisition, students must be assessed in a work context because skills are not enacted in isolation. This book contains a good introduction to the use of assessment for certification and in the validation of vocational education. (Note especially Appendix E, which is a synopsis of the Oklahoma Department of Vocational Technical Education Competency-Based Testing Program.)

U.S. Department of Labor, Office of Policy and Research. *Workforce Development Performance Measures Initiative: Final Report*. [www.wdsc.org/transition/measure/finalreport.htm]. July 1998.

This report offers the findings of a project. One goal of the project was to determine what measures could be used by a diverse set of constituents in employment, training, and education programs to track workforce development success. The second goal was to determine standard definitions for those measures. The main areas in which these measures would be used are basic adult education, occupational skills, and employment and reemployment skills. The final list of performance measures includes nine core measures (such as basic skill attainment and transition success rate), nine "other measures of success" (such as starting wage at entered employment and diversity of occupations), and six developmental measures (including return on investment and system penetration rate). Appendix C includes the detailed descriptions of the twenty-four performance measures.

Section V. Competencies Used for Overall Institutional Effectiveness

This section has as its focus the use of competencies by institutions for measuring how well an institution is meeting its goals. Included here are entries having to do with accountability, accreditation, and performance funding.

Accountability Processes

Note that the term *accountability processes* is defined here as statewide student testing programs and measures of quality.

National Center for Higher Education Management Systems. *The National Assessment of College Student Learning: An Inventory of State-Level Assessment Activities. A Report of the Proceedings of the Third Study Design Workshop.* Boulder, Colo.: National Center for Higher Education Management Systems (NCHEMS), Feb. 1996.

National Center for Postsecondary Improvement (NCPI). *Benchmarking Assessment: Assessment of Teaching and Learning in Higher Education for Improvement and Public Accountability: State Governing, Coordinating Board and Regional Accreditation Association Policies and Practices.* Stanford, Calif.: College of Education, Stanford University, National Center for Postsecondary Improvement, May 1997.

These two documents summarize statewide testing programs by state. NCHEMS's compendium includes the proceedings from a workshop, supplemented with documentation on "the extent and character of current state-level activities in assessing postsecondary student outcomes." These characterizations include descriptions of the origins and development of the state's program, assessment instruments used, obstacles to expansion of assessment activities, and what the state saw as the most "important needs to mov[ing] a national assessment agenda forward." NCPI also summarizes state assessment activities to include contact information and analysis of state assessment policy, including the policy context, policy type, and what stage the policy was in at the time of publication, guidelines, indicators, instruments used, and assorted additional information. NCPI also includes the work of regional accrediting associations in its review. Singly, each is a wealth of information; together, the two documents form a powerful reference on statewide assessment and testing programs.

Nordvall, R. C., and Braxton, J. M. "An Alternative Definition of Quality of Undergraduate College Education." *Journal of Higher Education,* 1996, 67(5), 483–497.

Nordvall and Braxton offer a response to traditional quality mechanisms built on reputational, resource, and value-added measures. They seek to drive the quality process back into the classroom and to the level of student engagement by using Bloom's taxonomy. Their approach rests heavily with faculty and eliminates student motivation issues that are a problem with assessments "added-on" to the curriculum. Although they never use *competency* by name in their ideas, they allude to it when they describe what they mean as "the level of understanding of course content to be demonstrated by students while engaging in course-level processes" (p. 486). A short discussion on the problems of aggregating course- and classroom-level information to the department and institution level is included.

Accreditation

Note that currently the Council for Higher Education Accreditation (CHEA) and the Western Association of Schools and Colleges (WASC) are working on standards that incorporate student competencies. See the earlier chapter by Dawn Geronimo Terkla for a full discussion of cooperative efforts to link competencies and accreditation.

Ewell, P. T. "Examining a Brave New World: How Accreditation Might Be Different." Speech presented at the Second Annual Council for Higher Education Accreditation Conference, "Enhancing Usefulness of Accreditation in a Changing Environment," Washington, D.C., June 1998. [www.chea.org /Events/Usefulness/98May/98_05Ewell.html].

Ewell focuses on the state of accreditation and how it might continue to evolve. Three main themes frame his talk: the revolution in teaching and learning, the "deinstitutionalization" of learning, and the need for public engagement. He calls for "examining the integrity of the degree" by using learning outcomes as the mechanism for this investigation. He notes that it is not merely whether the degree is of quality but also how resources and processes are "configured and used" to create a quality degree that must be considered. Practical suggestions for how to implement these ideas are given.

Teacher Education Accreditation Council (TEAC). *Accreditation Principles of the Teacher Education Accreditation Council.* [www.teac.org/principles .html]. n.d.

TEAC's three quality principles are evidence of student learning, valid assessment of student learning, and institutional learning. The cycle created by these three principles, if done well, incorporates the need to explicitly state what student learning is expected, how that learning will be assessed, whether the assessment is valid in the eyes of the program faculty (and presumably to the groups that employ their graduates), and how that information is used to improve the program in terms of "institutional learning."

Performance Funding

Burke, J. C., and Serban, A. M. (eds.). *Performance Funding for Public Higher Education: Fad or Trend?* New Directions for Institutional Research, no. 97. San Francisco: Jossey-Bass, 1998.

This volume is the most comprehensive and recent volume on performance funding. With regard to *competency-based* initiatives, however, it is rather sparse. A close reading of individual performance indicators reveals some measures that might nominally be linked to student competency. Some examples of potential indicators include "indicators of the effectiveness of remediation," "pass rates on professional exams," "job placement of graduates," and "employer surveys." They conclude that aggregating *individual* student competency and achievement to arrive at program or institutional measures of effectiveness has not yet been done effectively or equitably in performance funding.

Banta, T. W., Rudolph, L. B., Van Dyke, J., and Fisher, H. S. "Performance Funding Comes of Age in Tennessee." *Journal of Higher Education,* 1996, 67(1), 23–45.

This short historical profile of Tennessee's performance-funding process is linked to survey data collected from all twenty-three performance-funding coordinators in Tennessee. The survey focused on the usefulness of the various performance-funding measures. Competencies are not specified by the state, but they are implied by the use of general education assessment and major field-testing requirements in the performance-funding criteria. Survey respondents noted that even though these testing efforts have some effect on changing programs, it was also apparent that there is little motivation for students or institutions to take them seriously because no direct path exists linking competencies and assessments to student feedback and program improvement. (See also Banta, T. W. [ed.]. *Performance Funding in Higher Education: A Critical Analysis of Tennessee's Experience.* Boulder, Colo.: National Center for Higher Education Management Systems, 1986.)

Reference

U.S. Department of Education, National Center for Education Statistics. *Defining and Assessing Learning: Exploring Competency-Based Initiatives* (by E. Jones, R. A.Voorhees, and K. Paulson for the Council of the National Postsecondary Education Cooperative Competency-Based Initiatives Working Group). Washington, D.C.: U.S. Department of Education, National Center for Education Statistics, 2001.

KAREN PAULSON *is research associate at the National Center for Higher Education Management Systems in Boulder, Colorado.*

INDEX

Back Issue/Subscription Order Form

Copy or detach and send to:
Jossey-Bass, 350 Sansome Street, San Francisco CA 94104-1342

Call or fax toll free!
Phone 888-378-2537 6AM-5PM PST; Fax 800-605-2665

Back issues: Please send me the following issues at $27 each:
(Important: please include series initials and issue number, such as IR90)

1. IR _____

_____

_____

$ _____ Total for single issues

$ _____ Shipping charges (for single issues *only;* subscriptions are exempt
from shipping charges): Up to $30, add $5^{50} • $30^{01}–$50, add $6^{50}
$50^{01}–$75, add $8 • $75^{01}–$100, add $10, $100^{01}–$150, add $12
Over $150, call for shipping charge

Subscriptions   Please ❑ start   ❑ renew my subscription to *New Directions for
Institutional Research* for the year _____ at the following rate:

U.S.   ❑ Individual $59   ❑ Institutional $109
Canada: ❑ Individual $59   ❑ Institutional $154
All Others: ❑ Individual $83   ❑ Institutional $183

$ _____ Total single issues and subscriptions (Add appropriate sales tax
for your state for single issue orders. No sales tax for U.S. subscriptions.
Canadian residents, add GST for subscriptions and single issues.)

❑ Payment enclosed (U.S. check or money order only)
❑ VISA, MC, AmEx, Discover Card #_____ Exp. date_____

Signature _____ Day phone _____
❑ Bill me (U.S. institutional orders only. Purchase order required)
Purchase order #_____
Federal Tax ID 135593032   GST 89102-8052

Name _____

Address _____

_____

Phone_____ E-mail _____

For more information about Jossey-Bass, visit our Web site at:
www.josseybass.com   **PRIORITY CODE = ND1**

OTHER TITLES AVAILABLE IN THE
NEW DIRECTIONS FOR INSTITUTIONAL RESEARCH SERIES
J. Fredericks Volkwein, Editor-in-Chief